EARTH DIVINATION, EARTH MAGIC

EARTH DIVINATION, EARTH MAGIC

A Practical Guide to Geomancy

John Michael Greer

AEON

First published in 1999 by Llewellyn Publications

Aeon Books Ltd
12 New College Parade
Finchley Road
London NW3 5EP

British Library Cataloguing in Publication Data

A C.I.P. for this book is available from the British Library

ISBN-13: 978-1-91280-707-9

Typeset by Medlar Publishing Solutions Pvt Ltd, India

www.aeonbooks.co.uk

CONTENTS

ABOUT THE AUTHOR   vii

PART I: EARTH DIVINATION

CHAPTER ONE
The forgotten oracle   3

CHAPTER TWO
The figures   19

CHAPTER THREE
Casting the chart   55

CHAPTER FOUR
Reading the chart   67

PART II: EARTH MAGIC

CHAPTER FIVE
Geomancy and magic   115

CHAPTER SIX
Consecrating instruments   127

CHAPTER SEVEN
Meditation and scrying   139

CHAPTER EIGHT
Sigils and talismans   151

APPENDIX
A medieval handbook of geomancy   173

BIBLIOGRAPHY   185

INDEX   187

BLANK CHARTS   191

ABOUT THE AUTHOR

One of the most widely respected voices in contemporary occult studies, **John Michael Greer** is the award-winning author of more than fifty books, including *The New Encyclopedia of the Occult, The Druidry Handbook, The Celtic Golden Dawn,* and *Circles of Power: An Introduction to Hermetic Magic.* An initiate in Freemasonry, the Hermetic Order of the Golden Dawn, and the Order of Bards, Ovates and Druids, Greer served as the Grand Archdruid of the Ancient Order of Druids in America (AODA) for twelve years. He lives in Rhode Island with his wife Sara.

John Michael Greer is also the author of eleven fantasy and science fiction novels and ten nonfiction books on peak oil and the future of industrial society, and also blogs weekly on politics, magic, and the future at www.ecosophia.net.

PART I

EARTH DIVINATION

CHAPTER ONE

The forgotten oracle

Geomancy is a traditional Western way of divination based on intuitive contact with the subtle energies of the Earth. Nowadays, it's probably the least well-known of the major methods of divination belonging to the Western world's magical traditions; it's no misstatement, in fact, to call it the forgotten oracle of the West.

Even using the word "geomancy" in modern times risks a good deal of confusion. This term, which is derived from the Greek words *ge,* "earth," and *manteia,* "prophecy" or "divination," has come to be used in recent years for a flurry of different and mostly unrelated topics—from feng shui and related systems of spatial design, through ancient traditions of omen interpretation and prophetic lore based on earthquakes and other geological events, to speculations involving ley lines, megaliths, and hidden patterns embedded in the landscape. Each of these has something to do with the Earth, and something (although not always much) to do with divination; none of them have anything significant in common with the subject of this book.

From the high Middle Ages until the end of the Renaissance, by contrast, the word *geomancy* (and its equivalents in other Western languages) meant one thing only: a specific method of divination using a series of sixteen figures formed of points, and the philosophy and

3

practice centered on that method—a philosophy and practice based on a deeply magical understanding of the flow of elemental energies through the living body of the Earth. This same meaning of the word remained standard within the secret or semi-secret magical orders that carried on the traditions of Western occultism during the heyday of scientific rationalism, and it is the meaning that will be used here. This is not to dismiss the other traditions and teachings just mentioned; some of them deserve careful study on their own. The point that needs to be made here is simply that they have nothing to do with the kind of geomancy we will be discussing, and should not be confused with it.

A glimpse of geomancy

So what is geomancy? The best way to learn that is to see the method in action on a first-hand basis. As a first step in that direction, pick up a pen or pencil and a piece of paper. Think about a situation you are facing, one that is likely to have either a favorable or an unfavorable outcome, and then clear your mind and make a line of dots or dashes at random on the paper. Don't count the number of marks while making them. Do the same thing three more times, so that you have four lines of marks on the paper, like the ones below:

- - - - - - - - - - - - - - - - - - -
- - - - - - - - - - - - -
- - - - - - - - - - - - - - - - - - -
- - - - - - - - - - - - - - - -

Now count the marks in each line separately. If the first line has an odd number of marks, that equals a single dot • at the top of the geomantic figure you're producing; if an even number, that equals two dots • •.

If the second line has an odd number, put one dot as the next part of the figure, or two dots if the number of marks is even. Count the other two lines in the same way, to produce a figure made of four elements, each one a single or double dot. The result should be one of the figures in Diagram 1-1.

The favorable or unfavorable nature of the figure shows the most likely outcome of the situation. The meanings and symbolic name of the figure you have produced offer keys—some of the many used in more advanced approaches to geomancy—to the context of forces surrounding and shaping the situation and your place in it.

The traditional method of geomantic divination starts with four figures, not one, and then uses those four to generate a series of other figures that contribute to the meaning of the complete geomantic chart. Still, the process as you've just experienced it is geomancy in a concentrated form: using what we usually think of as "chance" to derive one of the geomantic figures, and then using that figure to cast light on a question or a situation.

The eclipse of geomancy

From a historical point of view, it's surprising that the art of geomancy needs even this much introduction. Geomancy was among the most popular of all divinatory methods during the last great magical revival in the Western world, the time of the Renaissance. Henry Cornelius Agrippa and Robert Fludd, two of the most important writers of that revival, both produced significant works on the subject. So did John Heydon, that master plagiarist of the English Renaissance magical scene, whose *Theomagia, or the Temple of Wisdome* contains a wealth of half-understood geomantic lore rarely touched since his time. These and other Renaissance texts drew on an entire literature of medieval European and Arabic works on geomancy, in which the basic techniques of geomantic divination had been expanded and applied in a vast range of ways.

Astrology was always the most important of medieval and Renaissance divination methods, because of its more extensive vocabulary of symbols and its deep connections to the way the entire universe was understood before the scientific revolution. Still, geomancy also had a significant role as a system of divination and a tool for thought. It made use of a great many astrological elements for its own purposes, and it may have been more commonly used as a means of ordinary divination.

The reason for this last point is not hard to find. In the days before computers, at least, the compilation of a horoscope required a substantial amount of paperwork and a solid grasp of mathematics, but a geomantic chart could (and can) be produced by anyone willing to learn a fairly simple process. This same simplicity makes geomancy perhaps the best introduction to traditional Western divination for the modern student.

Unfortunately, these advantages have been all but lost in the few modern presentations of the art. Unlike the medieval and Renaissance

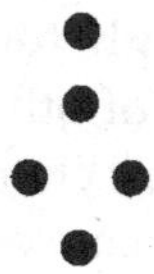

Puer (Boy). Rashness, violence, energy, destructiveness. Generally unfavorable except in matters of love and war.

Amissio (Loss). Transience and loss, things outside one's grasp. Favorable for love and for situations in which loss is desired, but very unfavorable for material matters.

Albus (White). Peace, wisdom, purity; a favorable figure, but weak. Good for beginnings and for business ventures.

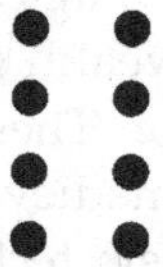

Populus (People). Multitude, a gathering or assembly of people. Good with good, evil with evil; a neutral figure, neither favorable nor unfavorable.

Fortuna Major (Greater Fortune). Great good fortune, inner strength. A figure of power and success, favorable for any form of competition.

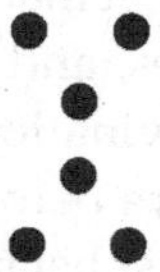

Conjunctio (Conjunction). Combination of forces or people; recovery of things that have been lost. A neutral figure, neither favorable nor unfavorable.

Puella (Girl). Harmony and happiness; a favorable figure in nearly all questions.

Diagram 1-1. The sixteen figures of geomancy. (*Continued*)

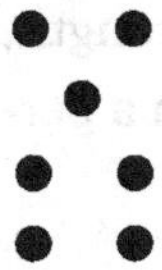

Rubeus (Red). Passion, power, fierceness, and vice. Evil in all that is good and good in all that is evil.

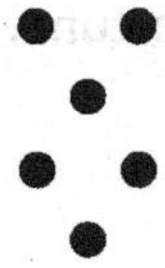

Acquisitio (Gain). Success, profit, and gain; things within one's grasp. Favorable in nearly all matters.

Carcer (Prison). Restriction, delay, limitation, imprisonment. An unfavorable figure.

Tristitia (Sorrow). Sorrow, suffering, illness, and pain. An unfavorable figure except in questions relating to building and the Earth.

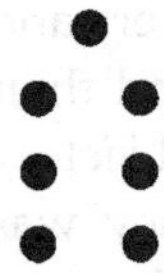

Laetitia (Joy). Happiness and health. A favorable figure.

Cauda Draconis (Tail of the Dragon). A doorway leading out. Favorable for losses and endings, but an unfavorable figure in most questions. Brings good with evil and evil with good.

Caput Draconis (Head of the Dragon). A doorway leading in. Favorable for beginnings and gain, neutral in other questions. Good with good, evil with evil.

Diagram 1-1. The sixteen figures of geomancy. (*Continued*)

●   **Fortuna Minor (Lesser Fortune).** Outward strength,
●   help from others. Good for any matter in which a per-
● ●   son wishes to proceed quickly.
● ●

●   **Via (Way).** Change, movement, alteration of fortune.
●   Favorable for journeys and voyages.
●
●

Diagram 1-1. The sixteen figures of geomancy.

methods, the forms of geomancy practiced these days are rigid, limited, and difficult to use effectively. The blame for this, surprisingly, must be laid at the door of the Hermetic Order of the Golden Dawn, the most important of the source groups behind the modern magical revival.

Founded in 1888, the Golden Dawn sought to collect the fragmentary legacy of Western magical practice into a single coherent system, and succeeded at this Herculean task as well as anyone ever has. In the process, the Golden Dawn's founders came across the half-forgotten art of geomancy and gave it a significant place in their Order's curriculum of esoteric studies. The Order's founders were better magicians and ritualists than diviners, though; furthermore, they were borrowers and synthesizers for the most part, rather than creative thinkers, and their treatment of geomancy betrays their limited approach to the subject.

The entire Golden Dawn "knowledge lecture" on geomancy was made up of a few basic instructions and some tables of general meanings for the geomantic figures extracted from Heydon's three-volume *Theomagia*. In their original context, these tables provided a general overview of certain aspects of the reading, and were meant to be supplemented and clarified by the more extensive discussions in the remainder of the text—as well as by the intuition and insight of the geomancer using them. All by themselves, though, these fragments of the complete system provide a badly distorted image of the process of interpreting a geomantic chart.

These problems have been amplified by the fact that practically all later works on the subject have taken the Golden Dawn version of the system (with or without acknowledgment) as their primary source, drawing little if anything from the other readily available sources—Agrippa and Heydon are only two of these—much less from the vast number of manuscripts on the subject, dating from the Middle Ages and Renaissance, that can be found in major European libraries. In most modern versions of geomancy, as a result, the interpretation of a geomantic chart has been reduced to a process of looking up cut-and-dried, arbitrary meanings from a set of tables. This is a sharply limiting approach at best, and one which offers far too little scope for the intuition of the diviner—which is, after all, the crucial factor in the whole process.

In the chapters that follow, we'll be exploring geomancy from a very different perspective. In place of canned answers from a collection of tables, we'll be treating the geomantic chart as a pattern of interacting meanings that can be grasped easily and quickly with the aid of a few simple guidelines, and interpreted through a combination of the figures' symbolism and the diviner's intuitive awareness. Although very few modern geomancers seem to have any knowledge of this approach, there is nothing new about it—a point that will be shown in detail in the appendix to this book, where I have given a short but complete medieval handbook of geomantic interpretation, *Modo Judicandi Questiones Secundum Petrum de Abano Patavinum* ("The Method of Judging Questions According to Pietro de Abano of Padua"), translated into English for the first time from the original fourteenth-century Latin text.

The origins of geomancy

As mentioned above, geomancy was a very common system of divination in medieval Europe, but it was not invented there. The first medieval books on geomancy were translated out of Arabic by Hugh of Santalla and Gerard of Cremona in the early twelfth century, and historians agree that the Arabs unquestionably had it long before that. It seems to have appeared in North Africa by the ninth century, and to have quickly become one of the standard systems of divination throughout the Arabic world.

Beyond this, however, there is little agreement. Persia, India, and the Arabic countries themselves have been proposed as the original sources for the art, but a careful look at the way it relates to other systems of divination suggests that the true origin lies elsewhere.

Geomancy belongs to a large family of divinatory methods founded on what modern mathematicians call binary or base-2 numbers.

The most famous member of this family is the I Ching, or Book of Changes, the most ancient and most important of the divinatory systems of China. (The link between these systems and binary numbers is a matter of history as well as structure; G. W. Leibnitz, the mathematician who first outlined the basic concepts of binary mathematics in the West, originally got the idea of base-2 numbers from studying early Jesuit translations of the Book of Changes.)

The principle underlying the whole family of methods is by no means limited to a Chinese context. It can be seen at work in the simple divination process of flipping a coin. Certain random or quasi-random events can be made to produce one of two definite results, and if meaning is assigned to the results, a clear answer can be found to any desired question. This principle has been used around the world in simple forms of divination, and in a few places it has become the foundation for more complex and informative approaches to divinatory work.

In consulting the I Ching, for example, the diviner tosses coins or shuffles yarrow stalks to produce six "heads" or "tails"—solid or broken lines, in this system—which are assembled, in order, into a *kua* or hexagram. With six lines, each of which can have two possible states, there are $2 \times 2 \times 2 \times 2 \times 2 \times 2$ or 64 possible hexagrams, and each of these has its own complex of meanings, with *moving lines* (determined by certain details of the divination process) adding another level of complexity.

Geomancy works in the same way, although it makes use of a smaller vocabulary of symbols. In geomantic divination, four heads or tails— single or double dots, here—are generated through the divination process to make up each figure. With only four binary digits to each figure, there are $2 \times 2 \times 2 \times 2$ or 16 possible figures, and these form geomancy's basic symbolic units of meaning.

It's worth noting that the vast majority of divination systems based on binary mathematics come from sub-Saharan Africa, and most of these use four binary elements, just as geomancy does. The simplest of them, which has been practiced over most of Africa for many centuries, involves simply casting four cowrie shells or half-nuts at the same time and noting how many fall face up or face down. Here no attempt is made to put the results into a specific order and create figures; the result of the divination simply depends on whether four, three, two, one, or no nuts or shells land face up.

More complex, and much closer to geomancy, is the *hakata* divination practiced by the Shona and other southern African peoples. Here four pieces of bone or wood, called *man, woman, boy,* and *girl,* and marked accordingly, are cast and used to produce one of sixteen figures. The same figures are produced in the West African *agbigba* divination method by the use of divining chains, which have four half-nuts that can spin freely to land face up or face down when the chain is cast; a set normally consists of four divining chains and is used to create four figures at once—another close similarity with geomancy in its Arabic and European forms.

The most complex of these African systems is the Ifa oracle of the West African Yoruba people, one of the most subtle and powerful methods of divination known anywhere in the world. Each of the Ifa *odu* or divinatory figures is made up of two of the sixteen basic figures we've been discussing, so that there are a total of 256 odu, each of which has a series of traditional verses assigned to it. A skilled *babalawo* (Ifa diviner) has memorized thousands of these verses, and works together with the client to select the verse most appropriate to the question once the odu have been cast. Here again, though, the intricacies of the Ifa system have been built atop the same set of sixteen figures used in so many other African methods—and in geomancy.

By contrast, there are very few systems of this binary type outside Africa. The I Ching has some degree of similarity, although it makes use of six binary elements rather than four. There is also a divination method from the islands of the South Pacific that uses eight binary elements. Then, of course, there is geomancy, which shares many structural elements with these various African systems of divination, and which first appeared in the Arabic countries of North Africa, at the other end of the caravan routes that connected sub-Saharan Africa with the Mediterranean and the lands around it.

It is just possible that the Arabic method came first, and the rich complexity of African binary divination methods evolved from it. On the other hand, this doesn't seem to have happened anywhere else geomancy has penetrated, and many African peoples themselves practice Arabic geomancy alongside their traditional divination systems, treating it simply as one more option for divinatory work. It seems a good deal more likely that geomancy has its roots south of the Sahara, and represents one of the major contributions of African cultures to the Western magical tradition.

The spread of geomancy

Whatever its actual origins, geomancy as we now know it reached the Arab world sometime prior to the ninth century. The Muslim conquests of the seventh and eighth centuries carried the Arabic language and culture as far as Spain in the west and Iran in the east, and once the fighting was over the conquerors quickly settled down and adopted much of the learning of their new subjects—a legacy that included most of what survived from classical Greek and Roman culture. For a period of several centuries, while Europe finished tearing itself apart into a patchwork of feudal kingdoms in which classical learning survived only in remote outposts such as Ireland, Arab scholars took up the legacy of the ancient world and became highly skilled in philosophy, mathematics, literature, science, and magic. Arab occultists studied alchemy and astrology, perfected the art of making magical talismans—in fact, our word *talisman* is derived from the Arabic *tilsam*—and practiced a wide range of divinatory methods.

In such a context, geomancy was bound to become popular. Its simplicity and flexibility quickly made it one of the standard approaches to divination throughout the Muslim world. It had numerous names; the most popular were *khatt al-raml*, "cutting the sand," and *'ilm al-raml*, "the science of sand," because most Arab geomancers used the desert sands as a convenient working surface to trace out the figures of the art. As Arabic culture spread in all directions, geomancy followed: east to Persia and India; south along the East African coast to Madagascar, where it was combined with local divinatory traditions to create the *sikidy* oracle; and north, finally, to the feudal states of Europe.

The first appearance of geomancy in Europe, as already mentioned, came in the form of Latin translations of Arabic texts in the early twelfth century. Modern historians have tended to stress the role of Arabic culture as a source of Western philosophical, medical, and scientific thought, but the same source also provided Europe with a large proportion of its occult lore as well. Works on geomancy came in along with texts on alchemy, astrology, and ceremonial magic, and all these were studied as eagerly as the treatises of Aristotle or Hippocrates.

As a result, geomancy quickly became a standard approach to divination throughout Europe; Lynn Thorndike, in his *History of Magic and Experimental Science*, has commented that geomancy "seems to have been nearly as popular in the medieval period as the ouija board is now." Poets could refer to geomantic figures by name without having to explain them, as Dante did in Canto XIX of his *Purgatorio*:

> ... and the geomancer sees
>   His Greater Fortune up the east ascend,

expecting his readers to know that Greater Fortune, the geomantic figure Fortuna Major, was connected to the Sun in astrological symbolism.

This same level of popularity continued unabated through the Renaissance. In the treatise of geomancy included in his encyclopedic *History of the Two Universes*—these being the universe around us and the universe within us—the English Hermeticist Robert Fludd recounted how in the winter of 1601–2, while spending a winter at Avignon in southern France, he performed a geomantic divination for a friend. As a result, he came to the unfriendly attention of the local Jesuits. When they went to the Papal Vice-Legate to accuse Fludd of practicing unlawful arts, however, the Vice-Legate dismissed the matter on the grounds that every cardinal in Italy relied on either astrology or geomancy; he himself, it turned out, was a skilled geomancer. A few days later, the Vice-Legate invited Fludd to dinner, and the two of them spent a pleasant evening discussing geomantic philosophy and practice.

This was admittedly an age when Francesco Patrizzi, a cardinal of the Church, could seriously propose to the Pope that the philosophy of Thomas Aquinas should be replaced with the magical writings attributed to Hermes Trismegistus as the foundation for Roman Catholic theology. Still, this very fact points out the extent to which Western magical traditions—geomancy among them—had penetrated Renaissance culture. That level of penetration remained intact until the entire culture of the Renaissance was crushed between the twin wheels of the Reformation and the Counter-Reformation in the seventeenth century, and modern materialist ways of thinking rose to their present dominance.

Chance, synchronicity, and meaning

Those very ways of thinking may make it difficult to see why the history just outlined traces anything but the rise and fall of a superstition, or why anyone should pay attention to geomancy today. Still, a closer look at what goes on in geomantic divination may cast some unexpected light on the subject—and on the weaknesses of ways of looking at the universe that most of us take entirely too much for granted.

The aspect of traditional divination that most often baffles people raised in modern Western culture is its habit of relying on what we call chance to answer the questions asked of a divinatory system. Most of the time, divination takes seemingly random factors—the number of birds that happen to come flying past at a particular place, the patterns made by leaves at the bottom of a teacup, the order of cards in a thoroughly shuffled Tarot deck, and so on—and uses these as the basis for intuiting patterns of meaning. Geomancy, as we'll see shortly, is no different; it uses a variety of essentially random processes to create the figures that the geomancer reads.

This reliance on the apparently random may seem strange or even pointless from a modern perspective, but this represents a weakness in our current models of the universe, not a weakness in the art of divination. What is chance, after all? As traditional philosophies around the world have always held, and as modern scientists working in fields such as systems theory and chaos studies are beginning to find out, nothing in the universe is actually random. What we call chance is simply the result of causes too subtle or too complex for us to break down into clear patterns and analyze by rational means. The entire universe, at all its levels, is linked by intricate patterns of cause and effect, and only the most blatantly obvious of these can be analyzed in any straightforward manner. The rest have to be intuited—and thus form a suitable subject for divination.

The psychologist Carl Jung used the term *synchronicity* to describe the subtle network of interactions or "meaningful coincidences" that shape the universe of our experience. The concept is much older than Jung, though, and it can be found in the teachings that underlie many of the world's systems of divination. If "random" events are not random at all, but rather the results of subtle patterns of cause and effect shaping the universe around us, one who learns to interpret such events can learn to read the patterns that shape them and go on to apply that knowledge to other events in the world of human life. The great advantage of "chance" events, in this context, is that they are less influenced by the more obvious currents of cause and effect, the ones that can be tracked and interpreted by rational means, and are thus more sensitive to the subtler patterns in the background.

From this perspective, it's worth noting, divination does not foretell the future; rather, it tracks the subtle currents of cause and effect in the universe, the rise and fall of patterns that favor or oppose various kinds of human activity. Some of these patterns can play a role in shaping events that have not yet happened, of course, and this allows a certain degree of insight into the future. In just the same way, someone who recognizes signs of approaching rain in the cloud patterns will have a certain degree of insight into the next day's weather. Equally, attention to the subtle patterns of cause and effect can lead the diviner to choose appropriate courses of action, just as someone who sees signs of rain in the skies may decide to carry an umbrella to work the next day.

To someone who has no knowledge of weather forecasting, the sort of insight this art can provide into future weather may seem supernatural. Similarly, the kind of awareness that is central to most kinds of divination can make it possible for the diviner to anticipate the future, and act on it, in ways that seem equally supernatural. In both cases, "supernatural" is precisely the wrong word. Divination, like weather prediction, is utterly natural. It depends on sensitivity to natural changes and attentiveness to pattern and flow in nature—but nature understood as a living entity and a context of intelligent powers, not the dead nature bound by rigid laws that is imagined by modern materialist science.

In turn, the practice of divination helps build the qualities of sensitivity and attentiveness to nature in those who practice it. In doing so, it opens the way to more profound and powerful ways of experiencing the world.

The soul of the world

The traditional philosophy underlying medieval and Renaissance geomancy does not use the term *synchronicity*, of course, but the basic idea is the same. To the geomancer of earlier times, the entire world was a pattern of meanings that could be caught by the perceptive eye and interpreted by the attentive mind. When birds flew past from a particular direction, when the stars and planets assumed particular arrangements, or when the chance patterns of a geomantic divination gave rise to a particular set of figures and their interactions, these things brought some part of that pattern of meanings into clearer view. They formed a page of what scholars and magicians called the "Book of

Nature"—a book that was the business of geomancers, among others, to read. It's the quest to attain this same sort of awareness that leads many modern magicians to seek, as one writer on magic has put it, "to treat every phenomenon as a particular dealing of God with my soul."

Fundamental to this idea, and to much of the inner worldview of the medieval and Renaissance geomancer, is the perception of the Earth as a living being. This is an all but universal concept among non-Western cultures, but it's not often realized that until the rise of modern materialist thought it was clearly understood in Western cultures as well. In the Neoplatonist philosophy that formed the foundation of the older Western way of looking at the world, all living beings were seen as a unity composed of three aspects—the *anima* or soul, the aspect of consciousness and essence; the *spiritus* or life, the aspect of energy and vitality; and the *corpus* or body, the aspect of material form. So, too, alongside the *corpus mundi* or body of the world (the physical world of matter we experience with our senses), traditional lore places the *spiritus mundi* (the essential life-energy of the world) and the *anima mundi* (the soul of the world, its consciousness and innate intelligence).

It's in the anima mundi, the inner side of the world, that the patterns perceived by the geomancer take shape as rhythms in the interaction of the four elements—Fire, Air, Water, and Earth—of ancient magical philosophy. These patterns then echo outward through the spiritus mundi to become visible to our ordinary senses in the realm of the corpus mundi.

A clear awareness of these patterns, then, makes it possible to sense how anything in the world influenced by them will form, develop, and pass away. The clear awareness that is needed comes through a combination of inward, intuitive attention, on the one hand, and careful observation of outward patterns on the other. The skillful geomancer learns to move back and forth between these two kinds of perception, bringing each one to bear on the other. By listening to the inner echoes of the anima mundi in his or her own awareness, and then relating these to their physical manifestation in the geomantic figures, the web of meaning communicated through the geomantic process becomes clear.

The way of the geomancer

The skills involved in this sort of work are uncommon ones in the modern world, to be sure, but they are within the grasp of anyone willing to put in the time and effort to learn them; geomancers are made, not born. The advantages of learning these skills start with the purely practical matter of having a way to sense the subtle patterns that shape so much of our daily lives. It's important to remember, though, that the advantages do not end there. Harder to define, but in many ways more important, are the effects of the regular practice of divination on the diviner: the growth of intuitive awareness, the development of sensitivity to the unseen, the establishment of a more balanced relationship between the individual self and the wider world.

The simplicity and clarity of geomantic divination make it, in some ways, the best choice among Western methods of divination for those who are first beginning to learn this approach to the world. The number of symbols to learn and master is much smaller than that of, say, the seventy-eight-card Tarot deck or the interlocking wheels of planets, signs, and houses that make up the alphabet of modern astrology, and the process of casting a geomantic chart is simple and quickly learned. At the same time, as we'll see, this simplicity does not keep geomancy from being able to communicate insights of great subtlety and complexity, or make it unsuited to the more advanced diviner. The methods of interpretation taught in traditional geomantic lore can be used at a wide range of levels, from the simple and basic to the complex and highly advanced; all of these are covered in the chapters to come, so novices and more experienced practitioners alike can find their appropriate levels within the broader system.

There are also further depths to the system, although these may not be of interest to everyone who decides to take up geomantic divination as a way of understanding the world. The same subtle connections of meaning in the anima mundi that make it possible to anticipate patterns of events also make it possible, in certain situations and by certain means, to shape those patterns. This is the foundation of magic. Magic is to divination what the hand is to the eye; it works with the same phenomena, but takes an active role rather than a receptive one. Although geomancy is not primarily a magical system, it does have significant connections to Western magical practice, and in some of the chapters to come we'll cover these in detail as well.

CHAPTER TWO

The figures

The alphabet of symbols used in systems of divination can range in size and complexity all the way from the simple yes or no of a coin toss to the 256 odu of the Ifa oracle and beyond. As just mentioned, though, the art of geomancy falls toward the simpler end of the spectrum. Sixteen figures, each one made up of four lines of either one or two dots, make up the fundamental alphabet of meaning in geomantic divination.

This is a source of strength in one sense, as it makes geomancy easier to learn and use effectively than many other, more complex systems. Handled in a simplistic way, on the other hand, this limited range of symbols might also make geomancy less effective at communicating fine details or tracing out subtle connections. Fortunately, geomancers down through the centuries have developed many ways of getting around the potential limits of a sixteen-element symbolic alphabet. As a result, there are a whole range of different levels to geomantic divination, reaching from basic approaches that provide broad general answers for the beginner, all the way up to subtle methods of analysis that make a geomantic reading as sensitive and informative as any method of divination in the world.

Much of the subtlety in geomantic divination comes in the actual process of setting up and interpreting the chart, which we'll be exploring in chapters 3 and 4. A part, though, comes from the fact that each of the sixteen figures connects to a rich body of meaning, much of it derived from links between the figures and other symbolic systems used in Western esoteric tradition, divination, and magic. These connections—*correspondences*, in the technical language of Western occultism—are in one sense learning tools that allow students who know one system to get a handle on another. On another level, though, systems of correspondences are a way to turn a simple, abstract image like a geomantic figure into an anchor for broad patterns of meaning rooted in experience, and they reflect the way in which everything in the universe of our experience mirrors the entire structure of the cosmos and of ourselves.

Correspondences of the figures

In this chapter, we'll be going through the sixteen geomantic figures and their correspondences in detail. The following correspondences are given for each figure:

Figure

The geomantic figures themselves are simple patterns of four to eight dots, which are generated by one form or another of the same odd-or-even process you experienced in chapter 1.

Elemental structure

Each figure is made up of four lines, and these lines are traditionally assigned to the four elements of Western magical philosophy—Fire, Air, Water, and Earth, in that order, from the top down. Ancient teachings hold that these four elements make up everything in the world we experience around us; modern scientists dismiss such ideas as pure superstition, but then go on to describe a universe made up of energies, gases, liquids, and solids—which is exactly the same classification in different words.

In the Western magical traditions that adopted geomancy, however, the four elements have certain aspects that a purely physical analysis doesn't cover. First of all, the Western magicians learned that the same four elements can be used as a language to talk about many of the less blatantly material parts of human experience. For example, they noted that the different functions of human consciousness—will, intellect, emotion, and sensation—relate to each other in much the same way that the four elements do, and they came to view the fiery will, the airy intellect, the watery emotions, and the earthy senses as the same elemental pattern expressed in a different context. Similarly, the directions, the seasons, the subtle flow of vitality in the human body, and many other things came to be seen as expressions of the same fourfold pattern at work in different contexts.

Second, Western magicians came to see that nothing in the world of human experience is made from one element alone. Even in a purely physical sense, a glass of clear water from the purest mountain stream contains Fire in the form of latent heat, Air in the form of dissolved oxygen and other gases, and Earth in the form of soluble salts extracted from the rocks of the stream bed. The same is true on less physical levels; even the most abstract of intellectual ideas, for example, will have traces of will, emotion, and sensation caught up in it.

It was by way of such realizations that the geomancers of the Western tradition came to see each of the sixteen geomantic figures as a pattern of interaction among the four elements, with the elements themselves understood according to the context of the reading. In these interactions, the elements may be active, focused, and obviously present, a state that is marked by one point, or they may be passive and dispersed, a state that is marked by two points. Each of the elements has a wide range of meanings—the elements themselves have correspondences, dozens of them, which can be studied in books on magical philosophy. In the most general approach to geomantic usage, though, Fire represents energy, purpose, and activity; Water represents form, receptivity, and the inner life; Air, which magical philosophy sees as the union of Fire and Water (what do you get when you put fire under a pan of water?), is interaction and relationship of all kinds, from the most harmonious to the most explosive; and Earth is manifestation, result, and material basis. Each of these factors, in turn, is either active or passive in any given geomantic figure.

Name

The name given for each figure is the standard Latin term used for it in Renaissance and modern handbooks of geomancy, with an English translation in parentheses.

Other names

Each figure has other names in some of the medieval and Renaissance handbooks of geomancy, and some of these offer useful clues to the figure's meaning. I have translated a selection of these under this heading.

Image

Each of the sixteen figures is, among other things, a simple picture made of dots. In a number of cases these pictures play an important part in building up patterns of meaning; they also make it easier for many people to memorize the figures themselves, which is an important step in learning geomancy and should not be neglected. The images given here are only one possible interpretation, and they can be expanded and altered in order to bring them closer to your personal sense of the meaning of the figure. Think of the figures as connect-the-dots pictures and the imagery will be clear.

Keyword

The core meaning of the figure as a divinatory symbol can be summed up in a single word, which should be memorized by the student and used as an anchor for learning and interpreting the figure's message.

Basic divinatory meaning

This is an outline of the most common meanings of the figures in actual divination, adapted from the material the Golden Dawn adepts borrowed from John Heydon's *Theomagia* and other sources, and expanded here with lore from the medieval tradition.

House relationships

The twelve houses, as will be shown in chapters 3 and 4, are the core framework for the more advanced levels of geomantic divination. Each figure has certain houses where it tends to be more strongly favorable, others where it tends to be more strongly unfavorable, and others still where it has a more powerful influence over the reading. These are given under this heading.

Quality

The sixteen figures are divided into eight stable figures (also called *direct* or *entering* in some texts) and eight mobile ones (also called *reverse* or *exiting*). Stable figures represent patterns and situations that are likely to last for some time, while mobile figures represent patterns and situations that will soon change. This set of qualities should be noted whenever time is a factor in a question, and some kinds of questions rely on this factor primarily.

Planet

Before the invention of the telescope, people knew of only seven celestial bodies that moved across the background of the stars: the Sun, the Moon, Mercury, Venus, Mars, Jupiter, and Saturn. These were called planets (from the Greek *planetes*, "wanderers") long before that term was given its present meaning. Other things moved in the heavens, of course—comets and meteors were known quantities, and the ancients were also aware of the precession of the equinoxes, a slow rotation of the Earth's poles against the backdrop of stars that shifts the entire sky a degree or so to the east every seventy-two years. Still, as the most visible moving bodies in the sky, the seven planets attracted a great deal of careful attention from ancient astrologers, and became symbols of great power as well; it's no accident that the planets are still named after divinities.

This same symbolism was applied to geomancy early on and, as a result, the attribution of planets to the sixteen figures follows the same pattern in nearly all the medieval and Renaissance texts. (The one variation was that the figures Puer, usually assigned to Mars, and Puella, usually assigned to Venus, were sometimes reversed.) Two figures were assigned to each planet, and the two left over—Caput Draconis and Cauda Draconis—were assigned to the nodes of the Moon, the points where the orbit of the moon crosses the apparent track of the Sun through Earth's sky. These latter points played a much larger role in medieval astrology than they do in most current approaches to that art. Generally speaking, the north node has some of the characteristics of Venus and Jupiter, the south node some of those of Mars and Saturn; at the same time, since the nodes are the points in the sky where eclipses take place, they share in the powerful and disruptive symbolism of these events.

Sign

Seen from Earth, the Sun appears to trace a circle through the starry heavens each year, and that circle—the ecliptic, as it's called, because eclipses only happen when the Moon crosses it—passes through twelve constellations. These are the origins of the signs of the Zodiac.

In contrast to the planets, which always seem to have been assigned to the geomantic figures in the same way, the signs have been associated with the figures in a startling number of ways, most of them contradicting each other and some of them contradicting themselves. One of the more straightforward systems, the one we'll be using, borrows the traditional planetary rulerships of the signs, as shown in Table 2-1.

Table 2-1. Planetary rulerships of the Zodiacal signs

Planet	Sign	Geomantic Figure	Outer Element
Sun	Leo	Fortuna Major	Fire
	Leo	Fortuna Minor	Air
Moon	Cancer	Populus	Water
	Cancer	Via	Water
Mercury	Gemini	Albus	Air
	Virgo	Conjunctio	Earth
Venus	Taurus	Amissio	Earth
	Libra	Puella	Air
Mars	Aries	Puer	Fire
	Scorpio	Rubeus	Water
Jupiter	Sagittarius	Acquisitio	Fire
	Pisces	Laetitia	Water
Saturn	Capricorn	Carcer	Earth
	Aquarius	Tristitia	Air

Outer element

Each of the figures contains all of the elements, as we've seen, but in geomantic tradition one or another element also has a dominant role in each figure. There are at least as many different ways of assigning the elements to the figures in this way as there are for linking the figures with the Zodiacal signs. Two of them seem to work well in divination. The first of these simply uses the elements that correspond to the Zodiacal signs just given. This set, which I have called the "outer elements" of the figures, has much to do with the way the geomantic figures express their energies in practical terms.

Inner element

The second set of elemental correspondences comes from the geomancer and magician Cornelius Agrippa, who provided several different systems but labeled this one an "esoteric arrangement." I have found that it does a good job of summarizing the dynamics of the elemental structure of each figure, and it can be thought of as the ruling element within each figure. I have made one change in the system as Agrippa gives it; he assigned Laetitia to Air and Rubeus to Fire, but I have reversed these in order to bring the inner element and the elemental structure into harmony.

Anatomy

Each geomantic figure corresponds to some part of the human body, a correspondence that was often used in geomantic medical diagnosis. The attributions given here are derived from astrological sources.

Appearance and character

Each figure also corresponds to certain physical qualities of the human body and to certain patterns of human behavior and outlook on the world, which allow the figures to identify people by a general description. This can be used in a range of specialized questions. It should be noted, however, that it's rarely a good idea to use a single figure to divine the appearance and character of the same person. Physical description and personal character don't necessarily have much to do with one another, and it's easy to make major errors by assuming that they do.

Colors

Traditional lore also assigns colors to most of the figures, and the few that are left out can be filled in by following the pattern of those given.

There are also four color attributions to each figure from the four Golden Dawn color scales, which are termed the King, Queen, Prince, and Princess scales for symbolic reasons. All of these are included as a help to certain magical uses of geomancy, which we'll be examining in chapter 5.

Commentary

The commentary to each figure, finally, is a brief meditation on the more important symbols, suggesting some directions in which the dance of symbolism around each figure might be understood. Just as a diver leaves the springboard behind in order to reach the water, these springboards to the imagination should be read, pondered, and then forgotten as you begin to find your way to a personal grasp of the figures.

●
●   **Fire: active**
● ●   **Air: active**
●   ●   **Water: passive**
●   **Earth: active**

Puer (Boy)

Other names: beardless, yellow, warrior, man, sword.
Image: a sword; a male figure with exaggerated testicles.
Keyword: strife.
Basic divinatory meaning: rashness, violence, energy, destructiveness. Generally unfavorable except in matters of love and war.
House relationships: favorable in the third house; unfavorable in the fifth; strengthened in the sixth.
Quality: mobile.
Planet: Mars.
Sign: Aries.
Outer Element: Fire.
Inner Element: Air.
Anatomy: the head.
Appearance: neither thin nor fat, with a short and solidly built body, brown or red coloration and often a very red face, small eyes, and uneven teeth; if bearded, the beard is sparse.
Character: troublesome, passionate, and excitable, with a tendency to start quarrels and stir up trouble, and an equally strong tendency to pursue sexual pleasure at the expense of all other considerations.
Colors: Traditional—white flecked with red.
     Golden Dawn King scale—scarlet.
     Queen scale—red.
     Prince scale—brilliant flame.
     Princess scale—glowing red.
Commentary: Puer is a figure of male sexual energy, balancing the feminine figure Puella. Unstable and forceful, it represents conflict, sudden change, and transformation, with all the constructive and destructive aspects these imply. Its astrological symbolism, Mars, Aries, and Fire, carries forward this pattern of meaning. Its elemental lines and inner element, by contrast, point to a deeper level of interpretation: Puer possesses energy and purpose, interactions with others, and a material

expression, but no receptive inner life. All the aspects of its nature are projected outward into the world of experience, as an act of creation or a source of delusion. Like a young warrior riding forth on a quest, it carries the spear of Fire, the sword of Air, and the disk or shield of Earth, but must seek the cup of Water elsewhere—an image that has more than a little to do with the inner meaning of the legendary quest for the Holy Grail.

```
        ●          Fire: active
      ●   ●        Air: passive
        ●          Water: active
      ●   ●        Earth: passive
```

Amissio (Loss)

Other names: grasping externally, outer wealth, something escaped or lost.

Image: a bag held mouth downward, letting the contents fall out.

Keyword: loss.

Basic divinatory meaning: favorable for love or in situations where loss is desired, but very unfavorable for gain. It often represents something outside one's grasp.

House relationships: favorable in the eighth house; unfavorable in the second; strengthened in the fifth.

Quality: mobile.

Planet: Venus.

Sign: Taurus.

Outer element: Earth.

Inner element: Fire.

Anatomy: the neck and throat.

Appearance: medium height, robust build, with a long neck, a large head, large shoulders and feet, a round face with a little mouth and attractive eyes. Tends to have a great deal of hair and at least one visible scar.

Character: frank and sometimes tactless, easily angered, deeply concerned with personal honor but sometimes given to lying.

Colors: Traditional—white flecked with citrine (a brownish yellow).
    Golden Dawn King scale—red-orange.
    Queen scale—deep indigo.
    Prince scale—deep warm olive.
    Princess scale—rich brown.

Commentary: Amissio is a figure of transience and loss, balancing Acquisitio's imagery of gain. Central to its meaning is a recognition of the hard truth that all things pass away. Its astrological symbols, Venus, Taurus, and Earth, point toward desire for material things as one of the classic examples of impermanence in human life; both the desire and the thing desired are certain to pass away in time, and so the experience of desire brings with it the certainty that the experience of loss will follow. Similarly, the elemental structure of the figure has Fire and Water alone; without Air to join them together or Earth to bring them into manifestation, these two opposed elements fly apart, and any contact between them is impermanent and without result.

```
 •  •      Fire: passive
 •  •      Air: passive
    •      Water: active
 •  •      Earth: passive
```

Albus (White)

Other names: (none)
Image: a goblet set upright.
Keyword: peace.
Basic divinatory meaning: peace, wisdom, purity; a favorable figure, but weak. Good for beginnings and for profit.
House relationships: favorable in the fourth house; unfavorable in the first; strengthened in the first.
Quality: stable.
Planet: Mercury.
Sign: Gemini.
Outer element: Air.
Inner element: Water.
Anatomy: the shoulders and lungs.
Appearance: larger above the waist than below it, medium height, with a large head, round face, small eyes, and a tendency to sweat easily. May have a thick beard.
Character: peace-loving, honest, and charitable, shy, tends to make many friends but to keep few of them, and to spend more money than he or she can afford.
Colors: Traditional—brilliant white flecked with red.
      Golden Dawn King scale—orange.
      Queen scale—pale mauve.
      Prince scale—color of new yellow leather.
      Princess scale—reddish gray tinged with mauve.
Commentary: Albus is a figure of peace and detachment, balancing the passionate figure Rubeus. Its astrological symbols, Mercury, Gemini, and Air, point to the way in which detachment has most often expressed itself in the Western world—the way of the intellect, which moves away from direct experience into abstract ideas. More deeply, though, Albus is a figure of Water, which is its only active line and also

its inner element; it represents the awareness caught up wholly in its own inner life and turned away from the action in the outer world of experience. In its highest form, this inward focus can lead the attentive mind to transcendence by the ways of mysticism, but it can also become a retreat from life that ends in sterility, isolation, and madness.

● ●   **Fire: passive**
● ●   **Air: passive**
● ●   **Water: passive**
● ●   **Earth: passive**

Populus (People)

Other names: congregation, multitude, double path.
Image: a crowd.
Keyword: stability.
Basic divinatory meaning: multitude, a gathering or assembly of people. A neutral figure, favorable with favorable figures and unfavorable with unfavorable ones.
House relationships: favorable in the tenth house; unfavorable in the eighth; strengthened in the third.
Quality: stable.
Planet: Moon.
Sign: Cancer.
Outer element: Water.
Inner element: Water.
Anatomy: the breasts and midriff.
Appearance: long and thin with narrow hips and a long face, dark coloration, and large teeth. Tends to have either a mark or blemish in or near one eye, or one eye of a different size or color than the other. Face is attractive and friendly, but body often unattractive. May have a thick beard.
Character: fond of traveling and never content to remain in a single place.
Colors: Traditional—green or very dark russet brown.
      Golden Dawn King scale—deep blue.
      Queen scale—sea green.
      Prince scale—deep olive green.
      Princess scale—white flecked with purple.
Commentary: Populus is a figure of dispersal and multiplicity, balancing the focused movement of Via. Its astrological symbols, the Moon, Cancer, and Water, are all images of passivity, reflection, and indirect action; they represent patterns of experience that have no direction or

focus of their own, but simply respond to energies coming from outside. The elemental structure of the figure shows all four elements passive and latent, but the receptive nature of Water comes closest to expressing the figure's nature in elemental terms. Like a crowd, Populus has no particular motion or direction until it receives the energy of another figure. Its stability is a function of sheer inertia rather than of any special strength of its own.

●   ●   **Fire: passive**
●   ●   **Air: passive**
●   **Water: active**
●   **Earth: active**

Fortuna Major (Greater Fortune)

Other names: inward fortune, protection going in, greater omen, inside or hidden help.

Image: a valley through which a river flows.

Keyword: power.

Basic divinatory meaning: great good fortune, especially in beginnings. A figure of power and success, favorable in any conflict or contest.

House relationships: favorable in the first, fifth, sixth, and eleventh houses; unfavorable in the seventh; strengthened in the ninth.

Quality: stable.

Planet: Sun.

Sign: Leo.

Outer element: Fire.

Inner element: Earth.

Anatomy: the heart and chest.

Appearance: thin and of medium height, with a round face, small teeth, and large eyes. One leg is often thicker than the other, and the face may tend toward a yellow color.

Character: Generous, modest, honest in speech, orderly and law-abiding, ambitious but with an easy manner. Sometimes tends to waste money in large amounts.

Colors: Traditional—green, yellow, or gold.
      Golden Dawn King scale—lemon yellow.
      Queen scale—deep purple.
      Prince scale—gray.
      Princess scale—reddish yellow.

Commentary: Fortuna Major is a figure of inner strength and resulting success, balancing the outer strength of Fortuna Minor. Its astrological symbols, the Sun, Leo, and Fire, are standard metaphorical images for strength and victory, but its elemental structure leads in some unexpected directions. Fire and Air are passive in this figure, with Water and

Earth active, and the inner element is Earth; like the valley that is its image, Fortuna Major represents a natural shape of events that brings success without apparent effort. Though we too often tend to think of success as a matter of vigorous action and struggle, real success comes about because our inner life is reflected in our outer circumstances (as it always is, for good or ill) without any conscious effort at all. This is one of the central secrets of magic.

```
●   ●     Fire: passive
    ●      Air: active
    ●      Water: active
●   ●     Earth: passive
```

Conjunctio (Conjunction)

Other names: association, gathering together.
Keyword: interaction.
Image: a crossroads.
Basic divinatory meaning: combination of forces, for good or ill, and recovery of things lost. A neutral figure, favorable or unfavorable depending on other figures and circumstances.
House relationships: favorable in the seventh, ninth, and tenth houses; unfavorable in the eighth and twelfth; strengthened in the first.
Quality: mobile.
Planet: Mercury.
Sign: Virgo.
Outer element: Earth.
Inner element: Air.
Anatomy: the intestines and belly.
Appearance: attractive or even beautiful, with a slender and delicate body of medium height. The face is long but attractive, with attractive eyes and a slender nose. The thighs are thin. If bearded, the beard is short and neat.
Character: intelligent and eloquent, luxurious, ingenious, dishonest, and unconcerned by legality. Tends to have many friends, and to spend more money than he or she has.
Colors: Traditional—purple or pale gray, sometimes black speckled
    with blue.
    Golden Dawn King scale—yellowish green.
    Queen scale—slate gray.
    Prince scale—greenish gray.
    Princess scale—plum.
Commentary: Conjunctio is a figure of contact and union, balancing the isolated and limited figure Carcer. It represents the union of opposites on all levels and the resulting potentials for change. Here the

astrological symbolism of Mercury, Virgo, and Earth ties into ancient magical images of fertility, and the elemental structure is open to energy in the Fire line and to manifestation in the line of Earth. Air and Water, the active elements in this figure, are thought of in magical philosophy as middle realms uniting the two ends of the elemental spectrum; Air, the inner element of this figure, also has a role here as a symbol of inter-action. Like a crossroads, Conjunctio forms a context in which move-ment can lead in unexpected directions and bring energies and people on highly different trajectories into interaction.

●   **Fire: active**
● ●   **Air: passive**
●   **Water: active**
●   **Earth: active**

Puella (Girl)

Other names: beauty, purity.
Image: a mirror; a female figure with exaggerated breasts.
Keyword: harmony.
Basic divinatory meaning: harmony and happiness; a favorable figure in most questions, but fickle.
House relationships: favorable in the fifth and seventh houses; unfavorable in the fourth; strengthened in the sixth.
Quality: stable.
Planet: Venus.
Sign: Libra.
Outer element: Air.
Inner element: Water.
Anatomy: the kidneys and lower back.
Appearance: attractive, plump, of medium height, with a long neck, round face, little mouth, attractive eyebrows and eyes, and large shoulders. Speaks in a pleasant voice.
Character: passionate, highly emotional, easily angered, intensely aware of his or her appearance. Falls in and out of love easily.
Colors: Traditional—white flecked with green.
　　　　Golden Dawn King scale—emerald green.
　　　　Queen scale—blue.
　　　　Prince scale—deep blue-green.
　　　　Princess scale—pale green.
Commentary: Puella is a figure of female sexual energy, balancing the masculine figure Puer. Puella is balanced and harmonious, but ambivalent. Its astrological symbols, Venus, Libra, and Air, suggest polar opposites held together in harmony and interaction by way of love, while its ruling inner element Water suggests that its energies are turned within, into a reflective inner life. The elemental structure is the key to this figure: with purpose and energy, inner receptivity, and the stability of a

material basis, Puella lacks only relationship and interaction to be complete. It seeks to unite with others, where its opposite Puer seeks only to be received—a distinction that has more than a little to say about the complexity of relationships between the sexes.

● ●   **Fire: passive**
●   **Air: active**
● ●   **Water: passive**
● ●   **Earth: passive**

Rubeus (Red)

Other names: burning, danger.
Image: a goblet turned upside down.
Keyword: passion.
Basic divinatory meaning: passion, fierceness, violence, and vice. Good in all that is evil and evil in all that is good.
House relationships: favorable in the eighth house; unfavorable in the second, fourth, and seventh; strengthened in the sixth.
Quality: mobile.
Planet: Mars.
Sign: Scorpio.
Outer element: Water.
Inner element: Air.
Anatomy: the genitals and reproductive system.
Appearance: strongly built, with red or brown coloration, a rugged face, and a wild and often threatening look. Often has a deep voice, and red spots or boils on the face. If bearded, the beard is thin.
Character: Hot, passionate, and fond of strong language. Tends to stir up trouble.
Colors: Traditional—red with brown flecks or streaks.
      Golden Dawn King scale—greenish blue.
      Queen scale—dull brown.
      Prince scale—very dark brown.
      Princess scale—livid indigo brown, like a beetle's shell.
Commentary: Rubeus is a figure of passion and involvement in life, balancing the abstract detachment of Albus. Its astrological symbols, Mars, Scorpio, and Water, are the standard images of passionate energy in the symbolic language of the heavens. Its inner element and the one active part of its elemental structure, though, are both Air. The lesson here is that passionate involvement in the world comes from focusing on how we relate to others and to the world itself. At its worst, this too easily becomes a blind intoxication with appearances, but it also has the potential to open the way to a loving participation in the experience of life.

● ●   **Fire: passive**
●   **Air: active**
● ●   **Water: passive**
●   **Earth: active**

Acquisitio (Gain)

Other names: grasping internally, inner wealth, something gained or picked up.
Image: a bag held mouth upward, as though to take something in.
Basic divinatory meaning: success, profit, and gain, something within one's grasp. Favorable in all material matters.
House relationships: Favorable in the first, second, and tenth houses; unfavorable in the seventh and eighth; strengthened in the eleventh.
Quality: stable.
Planet: Jupiter.
Sign: Sagittarius.
Outer element: Fire.
Inner element: Air.
Anatomy: the hips and thighs.
Appearance: medium stature, with a long neck, small ears, a small tense mouth, tense shoulders, and large eyes that have a tendency to look downward all the time.
Character: Timid, especially about money, but stubborn. Fussy about his or her appearance.
Colors: Traditional—red, yellow, or green.
　　　Golden Dawn King scale—blue.
　　　Queen scale—yellow.
　　　Prince scale—green.
　　　Princess scale—dark vivid blue.
Commentary: Acquisitio is a figure of gain and success, balancing the imagery of loss in Amissio. In its astrological symbolism, Jupiter is the traditional planet of good fortune, while Sagittarius and Fire represent energy directed toward goals. Its inner element and elemental structure stress that real gain of any kind exists only in a web of interaction, and seeks productive manifestation; all the money in the world is useless if no one will accept it in exchange, or if it simply piles up

untouched. The elemental structure also suggests the far from minor point that material gain, despite all its potential for interaction and material wealth, does not necessarily add up to the fulfillment of one's desires or the deepening of one's inner life.

●   **Fire: active**
● ●   **Air: passive**
● ●   **Water: passive**
●   **Earth: active**

Carcer (Prison)

Other names: constricted, lock.
Image: an enclosure.
Keyword: isolation.
Basic divinatory meaning: solidity, restriction, delay, binding, imprisonment. Generally unfavorable, but favorable for questions involving stability or security.
House relationships: Favorable in the fourth house; unfavorable in the sixth, seventh, eighth, and twelfth; strengthened in the twelfth.
Quality: stable.
Planet: Saturn.
Sign: Capricorn.
Outer element: Earth.
Inner element: Earth.
Anatomy: the knees and lower legs.
Appearance: medium to short stature, with a large head, short arms, dark coloring, strong chin, large chest, short thick neck, and round face with small eyes and mouth.
Character: fierce and passionate but magnanimous.
Colors: Traditional—white, russet, or dun (pale brown).
        Golden Dawn King scale—indigo.
        Queen scale—black.
        Prince scale—blue-black.
        Princess scale—cold dark gray, nearing black.
Commentary: Carcer is a figure of restriction and isolation, balancing the open and interactive nature of Conjunctio. This pattern of meanings has two sides, for restriction can be a source of strength and focus as well as a limitation. This is shown in its astrological symbolism, for Saturn, Capricorn, and Earth establish an imagery of rigidity and fixation, but also one of energy expended in productive work. The elemental structure develops the same theme: Fire and Earth represent energy and material expression, but they also remain at the two ends of the elemental spectrum, unable to come into contact with each other because neither of the middle elements are there to bridge the gap.

● ●   Fire: passive
● ●   Air: passive
● ●   Water: passive
●   Earth: active

Tristitia (Sorrow)

Other names: crosswise, diminished, accursed, head down, fallen tower, cross.

Image: a stake driven downward.

Keyword: sorrow.

Basic divinatory meaning: sorrow, suffering, illness, and pain. Unfavorable except in questions dealing with building and the Earth.

House relationships: Unfavorable in all houses except the fourth and eighth; strengthened in the twelfth.

Quality: stable.

Planet: Saturn.

Sign: Aquarius.

Outer element: Air.

Inner element: Earth.

Anatomy: the ankles.

Appearance: a long, thin, and unattractive body, dark coloration, large teeth, a long dark face, big feet, and rough unkempt hair.

Character: dishonest, unconcerned with legality, and prone to quick anger; slow to laugh, and even slower to forgive an injury or offense.

Colors: Traditional—tawny or sky blue.
      Golden Dawn King scale—violet.
      Queen scale—sky blue.
      Prince scale—bluish mauve.
      Princess scale—white tinged with purple.

Commentary: Tristitia is a figure of sorrow and difficulty, balancing the joyous symbolism of Laetitia. Its astrological symbolism is complex; Saturn has traditional links to ideas of pain and trouble, and these are reinforced by turbulent Air, but Aquarius carries meanings of creativity and benevolence that may seem hard to relate to this. The elemental structure and inner element stress Earth to the exclusion of all else, and this may also seem hard to connect. The deeper level of meaning these paradoxes resolve is simply that suffering is the one sure source of wisdom; too often, it's only when we are "stuck"—caught up in a painful situation we do not know how to resolve—that we learn to face the world in a wider and more creative way.

●   **Fire: active**
● ●   **Air: passive**
● ●   **Water: passive**
● ●   **Earth: passive**

Laetitia (Joy)

Other names: bearded, laughing, singing, high tower, head lifted, candelabrum, high mountain.
Image: a tower.
Keyword: joy.
Basic divinatory meaning: happiness and health. Favorable in almost all questions.
House relationships: favorable in the fifth house; unfavorable in the sixth, eighth, and twelfth; strengthened in the eleventh.
Quality: mobile.
Planet: Jupiter.
Sign: Pisces.
Outer element: Water.
Inner element: Fire.
Anatomy: the feet.
Appearance: tall and strongly built, with large feet, eyes, nose, and forehead. The hair is rough or disorderly, the neck thick, and there are often two prominent teeth.
Character: intelligent, honest, good-natured, and often very religious.
Colors: Traditional—glittering pale green.
        Golden Dawn King scale—magenta.
        Queen scale—buff flecked with silver-white.
        Prince scale—pale translucent pinkish-brown.
        Princess scale—brownish-gray stone.
Commentary: Laetitia is a figure of joy, balancing the harsh symbolism of Tristitia. It represents happiness of every kind and level, from the most momentary of passing pleasures to the highest reaches of human experience. In its astrological symbolism, Jupiter has its usual role as the planet of good fortune, and watery Pisces and the outer element, Water, represent the emotional life, the context in which joy is usually experienced. The inner element and the elemental structure generally, though, stress the role of energy in the attainment of happiness; it is by way of the free flow of creative force, in ourselves as in the universe, that joy comes into being.

●   **Fire: active**
●   **Air: active**
●   **Water: active**
● ●   **Earth: passive**

Cauda Draconis (Tail of the Dragon)

Other names: outer threshold, threshold going out, lower boundary, stepping outside.

Image: a doorway with footprints leading away from it.

Keyword: ending.

Basic divinatory meaning: an unfavorable figure in most questions, but good for endings and losses. Brings good with evil and evil with good.

House relationships: favorable in the sixth, ninth, and twelfth houses; unfavorable in the second, fourth, and eleventh; strengthened in the sixth and twelfth.

Quality: mobile.

Planet/Sign: south node of the Moon.

Outer element: Fire.

Inner element: Fire.

Anatomy: the left arm.

Appearance: more attractive from behind than from in front, with a long face, strong chin, long thin body, large eyes and teeth, and a long nose.

Character: corrupt and dangerous.

Colors: Traditional—green, white, dark crimson, or pale tawny brown.
     Golden Dawn King scale—glowing scarlet orange.
     Queen scale—vermilion.
     Prince scale—scarlet flecked with gold.
     Princess scale—vermilion flecked with crimson and emerald.

Commentary: Cauda Draconis is a symbol of endings and completions, balancing the symbolism of beginnings in Caput Draconis. Its astrological symbolism is that of the south or descending node of the Moon—the point at which the Moon crosses the Sun's path to go into the southern heavens. This point has some of the same symbolism as Mars and Saturn, the two malefics or negative forces in traditional astrology, and so Cauda Draconis symbolizes disruptions, losses, and endings. Its inner and outer elements are both Fire; the elemental structure, which lacks only Earth, suggests a situation nearing completion and thus ripe for radical change.

● ●   **Fire: passive**
●   **Air: active**
●   **Water: active**
●   **Earth: active**

Caput Draconis (Head of the Dragon)

Other names: inner threshold, threshold coming in, upper boundary, high tree, upright staff, stepping inside.
Image: a doorway with footprints leading toward it.
Keyword: beginning.
Basic divinatory meaning: favorable for beginnings and for profit. Otherwise, favorable with favorable figures, unfavorable with unfavorable ones.
House relationships: favorable in the second and seventh houses; unfavorable in the twelfth; strengthened in the fifth and eleventh.
Quality: stable.
Planet/Sign: north node of the Moon.
Outer element: Earth.
Inner element: Earth.
Anatomy: the right arm.
Appearance: medium stature, with attractive face and eyes, long nose, a large mouth, prominent teeth, and abundant hair.
Character: faithful, honest, and good-natured.
Colors: Traditional—white flecked with citrine.
    Golden Dawn King scale—citrine, olive, russet, and black.
    Queen scale—amber.
    Prince scale—dark brown.
    Princess scale—black and yellow.
Commentary: Caput Draconis is a figure of opportunities and beginnings, balancing Cauda Draconis' symbolism of endings. As the geomantic equivalent of the north or ascending node of the Moon, Caput Draconis shares much of the same focus on drastic change as Cauda Draconis, but the north node—the point at which the Moon crosses the Sun's path into the northern heavens—shares some of the symbolism of Venus and Jupiter, the two benefics or positive forces in traditional astrology. This figure thus represents change for the better, and is a particularly positive sign for beginnings. Earth, which is both its inner and outer element, and its elemental structure generally suggest fertile ground, needing only the energy of seed and sunlight; still, much depends on the seed that is planted there.

●   **Fire: active**
●   **Air: active**
● ●   **Water: passive**
● ●   **Earth: passive**

Fortuna Minor (Lesser Fortune)

Other names: outward fortune, protection going out, lesser omen, outside or apparent help.
Image: a mountain with a staff atop it.
Keyword: swiftness.
Basic divinatory meaning: favorable for anything that is to be done quickly. A figure of change and instability.
House relationships: favorable in the eighth house; unfavorable in the second; strengthened in the ninth.
Quality: mobile.
Planet: Sun.
Sign: Leo.
Outer element: Air.
Inner element: Fire.
Anatomy: the spine.
Appearance: heavily built, medium stature, with a round pale face, a very large nose, dark eyes, a large forehead, and a thick neck. Hair is thick, rough, and unkempt; if bearded, the beard is of medium length.
Character: bold, proud, and presumptuous, but generous, honest, magnanimous, and at times surprisingly humble.
Colors: Traditional—gold or yellow.
         Golden Dawn King scale—bright pale yellow.
         Queen scale—sky blue.
         Prince scale—bluish emerald green.
         Princess scale—emerald flecked with gold.
Commentary: Fortuna Minor is a figure of outer strength and success, balancing the inner strength of Fortuna Major. These two figures have the same astrological symbolism but the opposite elemental structure; they represent the same kind of experience—success—but have sharply different sources. Fortuna Minor represents success that is brought about by outside help or by circumstances, rather than by the innate strength symbolized by Fortuna Major. Easily gained, the success of

Fortuna Minor is just as easily lost, and it produces the best results in situations where rapid change is expected or desired. These factors are echoed in the symbolism by an unexpected shift in the outer element; Leo is a fiery sign, but Fortuna Minor is usually given the outer element of Air, representing the role of outside help in this figure as well as the instability of the results.

● **Fire: active**
● **Air: active**
● **Water: active**
● **Earth: active**

Via (Way)

Other names: wayfarer, candle, journey.
Image: a road.
Keyword: change.
Basic divinatory meanings: change, alternation between good and ill fortune. Favorable for journeys, but unfavorable for most other questions.
House relationships: favorable in the third, fifth, and seventh houses; unfavorable in the eleventh; strengthened in the third.
Quality: mobile.
Planet: Moon.
Sign: Cancer.
Outer element: Water.
Inner element: Water.
Anatomy: the stomach.
Appearance: medium height, tending toward fat around the middle, with pale coloring, small teeth, and a tendency to sweat easily. One eye is often different from the other, or there will be a birthmark or blemish somewhere near the eye.
Character: slow to anger but dangerous if roused. Loves to travel constantly from place to place.
Colors: Traditional—white flecked with blue.
　　　　　Golden Dawn King scale—blue.
　　　　　Queen scale—silver.
　　　　　Prince scale—cold pale blue.
　　　　　Princess scale—silver rayed with sky blue.
Commentary: Via is a figure of directed movement and change, balancing the diffuse and formless stability of Populus. These two figures, like Fortuna Major and Minor, share the same astrological symbolism but have opposite elemental structures. Here, though, the opposition is between complete passivity and complete activity. With all four elements

active, Via represents the elements in a constant state of change, each giving way to the next in an endless cycle. There is, however, a certain passive, reflective quality shared by these most opposite of figures. Despite the common figure of speech, roads actually go nowhere; it is the travelers who follow them that go somewhere, leaving more of the road behind with each step.

CHAPTER THREE

Casting the chart

The sixteen figures we've just explored make up the alphabet of geomancy. As with any other alphabet, though, the figures mean very little until they're put into a meaningful order and context. There are various ways to do this. It's possible to perform a basic kind of geomantic divination by simply producing one figure, the way you did in chapter 1, and reading the result as an answer. In traditional geomantic practice, though, a somewhat more complicated procedure is used. Four figures are produced by the workings of "chance," and then reordered and combined in specific ways to give rise to eleven others—and sometimes more, in the more advanced levels of interpretation. Although this longer procedure does take a little more time than the simpler approach just mentioned, it allows the figures to answer the question with much more than a simple "yes" or "no."

Questions for divination

Before beginning any kind of geomantic divination, though, it's necessary to settle first of all on a specific question that the reading will answer. The question provides the essential framework for the divination's meaning, the context in which the dance of symbols can be read and understood.

What kinds of questions can be asked and answered by way of geomancy? In medieval and Renaissance Europe, when the art was at its height, nearly any question imaginable might be the subject of a geomantic reading, including ones we would now answer through the use of very different resources. Weather prediction, for example, was a common reason for geomantic divination; the detection of thieves and the recovery of stolen property was another. People used geomancy to diagnose diseases, decide on routes for journeys, check the accuracy of news or rumors from distant places, choose strategies for warfare and other contests, find missing persons, test for pregnancy, and much more. Any question that could not be answered on the basis of solid knowledge could be explored through the less certain but still valuable resource of geomancy. Nowadays there are more reliable ways to check on many of these things, but the world still has plenty of unknown and unpredictable factors at work, and geomancy can be used to provide insight into the way these will work out in almost any area of human life.

Whatever the subject of the divination, though, the question needs to be thought out and phrased clearly before the process begins. There's little value in looking for an answer before you've made sure of the question! Take the time to think through the different aspects of the question, and to formulate it in a single sentence if at all possible. It can be useful, especially when the issues are unusually complex or emotionally difficult, to write down all the factors you know about—those helping you deal with the situation as well as those hindering you— and search for common patterns. These will often appear in the reading itself as specific symbols, and the more you know about them the more readily you will recognize them and trace their interactions.

Equipment for divination

Once the question has been settled, the next step in geomantic divination involves generating a set of four figures by some random or quasi-random method. There are several different ways to do this, but far and away the most traditional is to take a sharpened stick and make a line of marks in the ground. This is done while the geomancer's mind is still focused on the question, and the number of marks is not counted while they are being made. The geomancer then goes on to make a second line, a third, and so on, until sixteen lines of marks have been made.

In earlier times, when the vast majority of people lived in rural settings, it was much easier to find a conveniently flat surface of sand or earth for this purpose, and to make use of it without anyone else being the wiser. (The deserts of North Africa and the Middle East were perfect for the purpose—an important reason, quite possibly, why geomancy became so popular so quickly in those lands.) In urban environments, this can be a more difficult prospect, both because there is so much less bare soil and because there are so many more people who might interrupt the process. For this reason, several other options have been devised.

Probably the best of these is to make or obtain a wide, shallow wooden box and fill it halfway with sand or earth, as shown in Diagram 3-1. A thin wooden wand with a pointed end—a length of narrow dowel will serve—is then used to mark the surface and produce the figures. The box should be sealed on the bottom and sides to keep its contents from sifting out; caulk or waterproof glue can be used for this purpose,

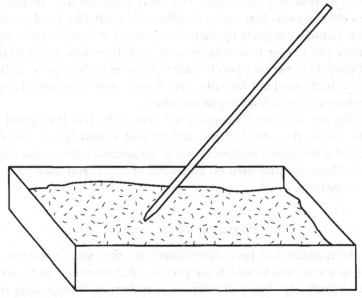

Diagram 3-1. Box, sand, and wand.

but metal foil should be avoided as it cuts off the box from the flow of terrestrial energies.

Another approach, which was also in common use throughout the Middle Ages, was to replace the sand and divining wand with a sheet of parchment and a quill pen. Plain paper and a pencil or ballpoint pen will work just as well.

There are at least three other ways to accomplish the first step of geomantic divination; although somewhat less traditional, they are admittedly easier to use in a modern urban or suburban setting. The first of these involves a bowl or cloth bag of small stones. The diviner takes or pours out a random number of the stones into one hand; the stones are then counted, and the number—odd or even—determines the number of points in each element of a geomantic figure.

The second of these alternate ways is to have a set of four coins or flat sticks, marked with one dot on one side and two dots on the other. These are tossed up in the air, and the way they land determines the nature of an entire figure all at once. The coins or sticks will also have to be marked in some way so that you can tell which one makes which line of the figure you are casting; a number mark or a color code based on the elements (red for Fire, yellow for Air, blue for Water, green for Earth) is a good way to do this. The third alternate way, finally, is to make a deck of cards that can be shuffled and dealt, like Tarot cards. It's possible to put a complete figure on each card, but it can be more useful to simply put one or two dots on each, and draw four cards to make each figure. In either case you'll want to have enough cards of each sort so that you can deal out four identical figures; this sometimes happens and, when it does, it is an important omen.

Finally, you will need a copy of the first of the two traditional geomantic charts, the shield chart, and (if you intend to use the more advanced interpretive methods) one of the second—the house chart—as well. These are provided on pages 223 and 224, and may be copied for personal use.

Preparing for divination

Once the question has been determined, the next step is to enter into a state of awareness in which the process of divination can be accomplished effectively. The basic requirement here is the opening up of contact between the consciousness of the diviner and the wider consciousness of the anima mundi.

This is both easier and more difficult than it may sound. On the one hand, magical philosophy holds (and the experience of magical practice quickly shows) that there are no sharp divisions in the realm of consciousness. Each conscious being, human or not, is a pattern in the flow of consciousness, a center where consciousness gathers and deepens and then passes on. It's through this unifying flow of awareness that fads and a variety of other mass phenomena pass from mind to mind, and through the same flow that human beings naturally connect to the broader consciousness of the universe as a whole.

On the other hand, many of the common habits of human thought, and in particular many of the ways people in the West are taught to use their minds, get in the way of this natural linkage to the flow of consciousness. The task of the geomancer is to get these impediments out of the way. This is simple enough—but "simple," of course, is not always the same thing as "easy."

The necessary shift in awareness can be made in a number of different ways, ranging from the simple act of clearing the mind to complex ritual processes drawn from the lore of ceremonial magic. In this chapter, an example of the simpler kind will be given, while two other more complex methods will be provided in chapter 5. Any one of them, given effort and practice, will do what needs to be done; some people will find that one or another method works best for them, while others may find all three equally effective. It's also possible, and appropriate, to devise a method of your own, which may well draw on whatever magical or spiritual system you personally find best suited to the work. Here, as so often, the personal equation is the deciding factor.

A basic method of preparing for geomantic divination is simply to close your eyes and draw your attention inward, focusing your mind on the question you seek to answer. Don't think about the question, in the usual sense of the phrase; instead, hold the question itself in your mind, keeping your thoughts fixed on it, leaving the whole array of potential consequences, worries, hopes, and fears outside. Let your awareness settle into place, and allow all other issues to fade from the center of attention. When you are able to focus yourself in this way, begin the divination process.

Whatever approach you choose, the old texts stress that it is unwise to attempt divination when the diviner's mind is troubled by anger or worry, because disturbances of this kind will get in the way of the interaction that needs to take place between the diviner's awareness and that of the universe. While performing the first steps of the divination, especially, it is vitally important to set aside hopes and fears about the outcome of the divination, and simply allow the figures to take shape as they will.

Some of the medieval and Renaissance geomancy textbooks also suggest that it is unwise to try to perform a geomantic divination when the weather is unsettled, or when there is any great amount of wind or rain. The idea behind this is that a stormy day is to the anima mundi more or less what a stormy mood is to the diviner, and will confuse the divination in the same way. Other writers deny that this has any effect at all, though, and my own experience seems to agree with this. You may nevertheless wish to keep track of the weather conditions during any particular divination, and compare the accuracy of your readings in stormy and sunny weather; the personal equation may be a major factor here as well.

Generating the Four Mothers

Once the preparation has been completed, the next step is to produce four geomantic figures using whatever geomantic equipment you have chosen. This requires sixteen different odd or even results.

In the classical method, for example, the diviner makes a set of sixteen lines of dots in the sand with his or her wand. The number of dots in the first line are then counted, just as you did in chapter 1; an odd number gives a single dot, an even result two dots, and this is taken as the head or Fire line of the first figure. The second line produces the neck or Air line, the third the body or Water line, and the fourth the feet or Earth line of the first figure. The fifth line produces the head of the second figure, and so on. The sixteen lines thus produce four geomantic figures, which are called the Four Mothers. An example of the entire process is shown in Diagram 3-2.

Generating the Four Daughters

Once you have the Four Mothers, the first phase of geomantic divination is over, and the wand, paper, stones, coins, or cards can be put away. The next four figures, the Four Daughters, are generated from the Mothers by a simple process of rearrangement. The First Daughter is produced by taking the head of each of the Four Mothers in order: thus

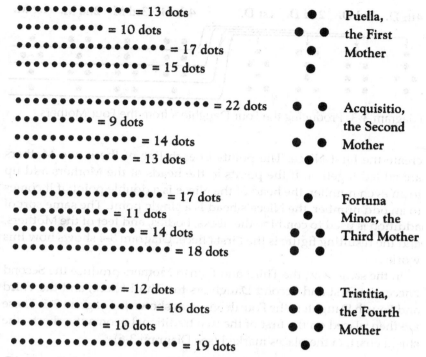

●●●●●●●●●●●●● = 13 dots   ●   Puella,
●●●●●●●●●● = 10 dots   ● ●   the First
●●●●●●●●●●●●●●●●● = 17 dots   ●   Mother
●●●●●●●●●●●●●●● = 15 dots   ●

●●●●●●●●●●●●●●●●●●●●●● = 22 dots ● ●   Acquisitio,
●●●●●●●●● = 9 dots   ●   the Second
●●●●●●●●●●●●●● = 14 dots   ● ●   Mother
●●●●●●●●●●●●● = 13 dots   ●

●●●●●●●●●●●●●●●●● = 17 dots   ●   Fortuna
●●●●●●●●●●● = 11 dots   ●   Minor, the
●●●●●●●●●●●●●● = 14 dots   ● ●   Third Mother
●●●●●●●●●●●●●●●●●● = 18 dots   ● ●

●●●●●●●●●●●● = 12 dots   ● ●   Tristitia,
●●●●●●●●●●●●●●●● = 16 dots   ● ●   the Fourth
●●●●●●●●●● = 10 dots   ● ●   Mother
●●●●●●●●●●●●●●●●●●● = 19 dots   ●

Diagram 3-2. An example of how the Four Mothers are produced.

the head of the First Mother becomes the First Daughter's head; the head of the Second Mother becomes the First Daughter's neck; the head of the Third Mother becomes the First Daughter's body, and the head of the Fourth Mother becomes the First Daughter's feet. In the same way, the necks of the Mothers produce the Second Daughter, their bodies the Third Daughter, and their feet the Fourth Daughter, as shown in Diagram 3-3.

Generating the Four Nieces

At this point a third process comes into play to create what the medieval handbooks called the Four Nieces (in modern books on geomancy, these are usually called the Four Nephews). We can demonstrate with the First and Second Mothers, which are combined to

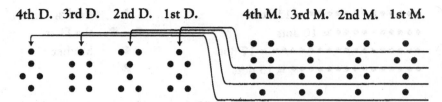

4th D.   3rd D.   2nd D.   1st D.   4th M.   3rd M.   2nd M.   1st M.

Diagram 3-3. Producing the Four Daughters from the Four Mothers.

create the First Niece. The points in each line of these two Mothers are added together. If the points in the heads of the Mothers add up to an even number, the head of the Niece is a double point; if it comes to an odd number, the Niece's head is a single point. The same sort of addition is used to combine the necks, bodies, and feet of the Mothers, and the resulting figure is the First Niece. Diagram 3-4 shows how this works.

In the same way, the Third and Fourth Mothers produce the Second Niece, the First and Second Daughters the Third Niece, and the Third and Fourth Daughters the Fourth Niece, as shown in Diagram 3-5. These are then placed on the first of the two traditional geomantic charts, the shield chart, in the places marked (see Diagram 3-6).

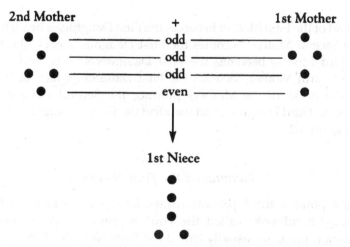

Diagram 3-4. Producing the First Niece from the First and Second Mothers.

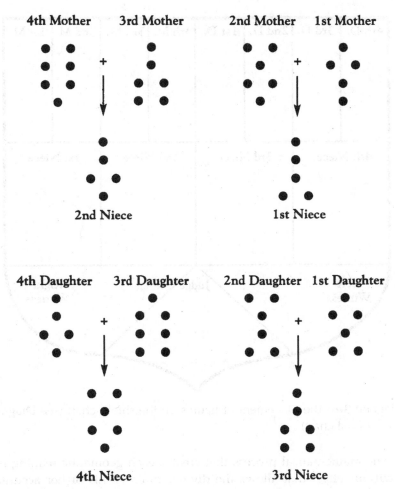

Diagram 3-5. Producing the Four Nieces.

Generating the Witnesses and Judge

The same additive process that produces the Nieces is continued further, giving rise to three more figures: the Witnesses and the Judge. The Right Witness is created by adding together the First and Second Nieces, the Left Witness by adding together the Third and Fourth Nieces. Finally, the Judge is created by adding together the Witnesses according to the same process. The complete process is shown in Diagram 3-7.

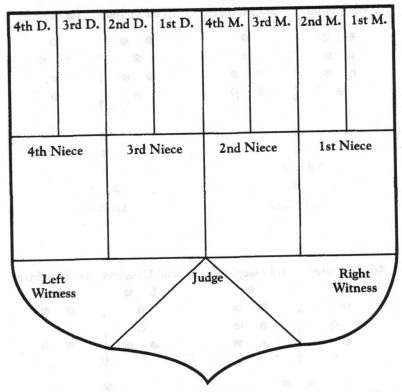

Diagram 3-6. The placement of figures on the shield chart (see Diagram 3-7 for final chart).

The mathematical process that creates each geomantic reading has a curious effect that allows the diviner to check his or her accuracy. Since the same points differently arranged make up the Mothers and the Daughters, the Judge—the only figure generated from both sides of the reading—will always have an even number of points making it up. As a result, only eight of the sixteen figures—Amissio, Populus, Fortuna Major, Conjunctio, Carcer, Acquisitio, Fortuna Minor, and Via—can be the Judge in a reading. If you get any other figure for the Judge, you need to go back and double check your addition.

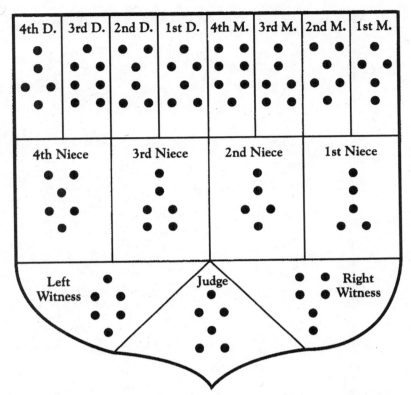

Diagram 3-7. A complete chart, including the Judge and Witnesses.

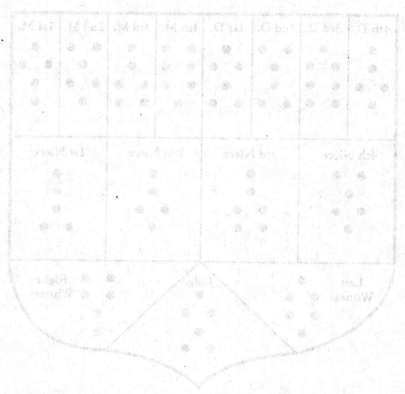

Diagram 3-1. A complete chart, including the Judge and Witnesses.

CHAPTER FOUR

Reading the chart

B y the end of the process described in chapter 3, you will have generated the complete set of geomantic figures you'll need for a reading, and the mechanical part of geomantic divination is finished. What remains is the interpretation of the chart, where the patterns that have come out of this first phase become bearers of meaning.

The process of interpretation has had far too much mystery built up around it. In an important sense, it's simply a matter of telling a story, one in which the geomantic figures are the basic plot elements and the *querent*—the person for whom the divination has been done, whether this is the diviner or someone else—is the main character. The theme and the setting for the story are provided, for the most part, by the question the divination is meant to answer. This shouldn't be taken too rigidly, though; human lives and human motivations are complex things, and apparently straightforward questions may lead off in directions you don't expect.

In putting together the story told by the figures, of course, the most important guide is the intuition of the diviner. This is one of the chief reasons why using charts and tables to interpret a geomantic reading is so unsatisfactory. The figures that come together in a divination reflect the living pattern of forces at work in some part of the querent's life, not simply a set of rigid answers from a table. It's because of this that each diviner comes to understand the symbols of his or her art in a slightly different way from anyone else.

The witnesses and the judge

As mentioned before, there's more than one way to read a geomantic divination, depending on the level of detail that is needed and the level of skill the diviner has reached. As you begin to learn the art of geomantic divination, it's a good idea to start off with the most basic methods of interpreting a chart, master those, and then move on to the more complex ones. To this end, the interpretive methods that will be covered in this chapter have been given in their approximate order of difficulty so that they may be studied and learned in order.

The first and most basic level of interpretation makes use of the relationships among the Witnesses and the Judge. Of these, the Judge itself is far and away the most significant, and it's possible to get a fairly clear idea of the basic outlines of the reading by taking the Judge alone as a guide. If the question that has been asked can be answered with a "yes" or "no," a favorable Judge means yes, an unfavorable one no. A more complex question often finds its answer in more specific details of the meaning of the figure that appears as Judge.

The two Witnesses, the figures from which the Judge is produced, add an additional level of meaning. A favorable Judge derived from two favorable Witnesses is made more positive still, while an unfavorable Judge derived from two unfavorable Witnesses is the worst possible sign. A Judge, favorable or unfavorable, which is produced from one favorable and one unfavorable Witness, takes on a middle significance, representing a situation in which good and ill are combined. A favorable Judge coming from this combination often means success, but with difficulty and delay; an unfavorable Judge from the same situation often means failure, but with some mitigating factors.

A favorable Judge derived from two unfavorable Witnesses becomes unfavorable, although not extremely so; it often means a seemingly positive turn of events that comes out less than positively in the long run. An unfavorable Judge derived from two favorable Witnesses becomes somewhat favorable, and can often mean a negative outcome that has important positive effects on other things. In all cases, the meaning of the figures themselves should be carefully studied, as these provide the context in which these favorable or unfavorable indications take shape.

There is also the element of time in these relationships. The Right Witness is said to represent the question's past, and the Left Witness the question's future, while the Judge represents the present situation. Thus, for example, a favorable Judge derived from an unfavorable Right Witness and a favorable Left Witness represents a turn for the better, in which past difficulties are left behind; the same Judge derived from a favorable Right Witness and an unfavorable Left Witness stands for a situation in which past and present successes will be paid for with future trouble.

Sample readings

A few examples will help make these relationships clearer.

Sample reading 1

Diagram 4-1 shows the first of these. The querent invested much of her money in a small business, and lost a great deal of it when a pipe burst in her store and most of the inventory was ruined. She wants to know if she should borrow money and restock or just pay off her remaining debts and close the store.

The chart, which has Cauda Draconis for the Right Witness and Laetitia for the Left Witness, has Conjunctio as Judge. Cauda Draconis is an unfavorable, disruptive figure, good only for losses and endings; it very likely refers to the situation brought about by the bursting pipe. Laetitia is favorable in almost any question. The judge, Conjunctio, is a neutral figure, meaning a combination of forces for good or ill; under the influence of the Witnesses, it keeps this neutral quality.

Factoring in the element of time, this combination shows a pattern of events in which the querent has suffered a significant loss in the past, but as a result of a combination of factors in the present, the future is very bright indeed. She should certainly refinance and stay in business, and she should also be open to the possibility of unexpected combinations—for example, taking on a partner or an investor.

Sample reading 2

The second reading is shown in Diagram 4-2. The querent is a college student pursuing a master's degree. The degree program is proving more difficult and time-consuming than he had expected, and he

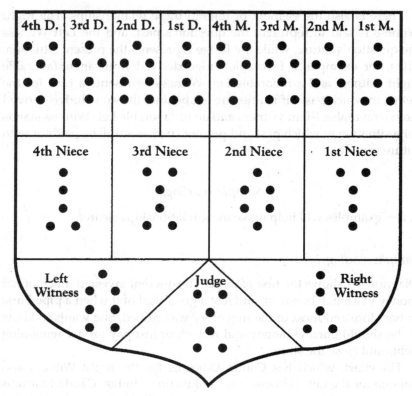

Diagram 4-1. Sample reading 1.

is thinking about dropping it and trying some less demanding field. He wants to know what the outcome would be if he did so.

Here Puella is the Right Witness and Albus is the Left, with Carcer for the Judge. Carcer is normally a sharply unfavorable figure, but under the influence of two favorable Witnesses it becomes somewhat favorable. Its basic meaning of limitation, however, does not change, and it represents a course of action which, while successful over the short term, places limits on what can be achieved in a broader sense. Puella and Albus are both somewhat passive figures, and the whole pattern suggests that the querent is taking the easy way out, and choosing present happiness and comfort at the expense of his long-term potential. On the other hand, Albus as a symbol of the future does suggest that he will do tolerably well in a less demanding career.

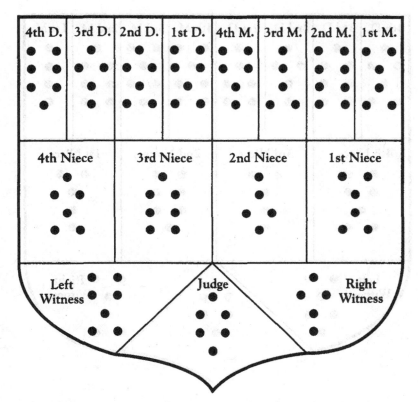

Diagram 4-2. Sample reading 2.

Sample reading 3

The third reading is shown in Diagram 4-3. The querent, an artist who has just graduated from art school, is trying to place a number of her sculptures at an important local gallery. Her presentation to the gallery owners seems to have gone well, but she is still waiting for their final decision. A great deal depends on the question, for a successful show at this point could effectively make her career.

In this reading the Right Witness is Conjunctio, the Left Witness Acquisitio, and the Judge Fortuna Major. Conjunctio is a neutral figure, meaning a combination of forces, while Fortuna Major and Acquisitio are among the best of the sixteen figures. Conjunctio, representing the past, very likely stands for her contacts with the gallery owners;

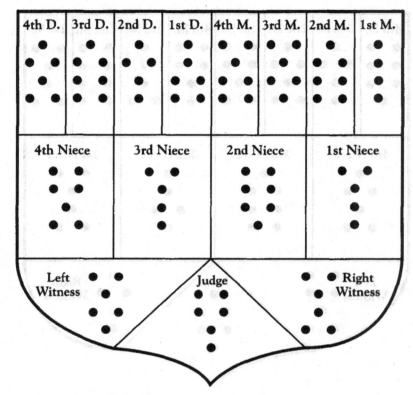

Diagram 4-3. Sample reading 3.

Fortuna Major, as the present situation, suggests that her work will indeed be shown, while Acquisitio, as the future, predicts that the show will be a success.

The way of the points

Another basic tool for interpreting a geomantic chart allows the diviner to find out the root of the question—the factor which, often unknown to the querent, is the driving force behind the whole situation. This is determined by a method known as the Way of the Points.

The Way of the Points is traced out on the complete geomantic chart, starting with the Judge. Look at the first element, the head or Fire line of the Judge, and note whether that element is a single or a double point. Then go to the Witnesses, and see if either of these has the same first line.

If the Way of Points cannot be formed—as in Diagram 4-1, where the Judge has a double point as its head, but each of the Witnesses has a single point—this suggests that the situation is exactly what it seems. If one of the Witnesses has the same head as the Judge, though, the Way of the Points moves from the Judge to that Witness.

From here the same process is repeated, and the two Nieces that generated the Witness in question are checked to see if either has the same first line. If so, the Way of the Points goes to that Niece; if not, it stops at the Witness. From the Niece, the Way goes to the Daughters or Mothers, depending on which Niece is involved, and once again the two figures that generated the Niece are checked to see if either or both of them share the same first line.

The figure or figures where the Way of the Points comes to an end, whether the Judge, a Witness, a Niece, or a Daughter or Mother, represent the root factor or factors of the situation, and should be taken as a guide to the inner nature of the question and the true driving force behind it.

It's worth noting that if the Fire line of the Judge is a single point, the Way of Points will always be formed, and will always follow an unbranching path up to one of the Mothers or Daughters. If the Judge's Fire line is a double point, on the other hand, the Way of Points—if it forms at all—will always branch and end at more than one figure. In exceptional cases, it can include every figure in the chart! This difference is a result of the way the lower figures are generated, but it also represents a source of insight. Of the eight figures that can be the Judge, four—Amissio, Carcer, Fortuna Minor, and Via—begin with a single point, and four—Populus, Fortuna Major, Conjunctio, and Acquisitio—begin with a double point. Situations of the sort described by the first four often have a single root cause, whether or not this is visible at first glance. Situations of the sort described by the second four, on the other hand, often have more diffuse causes.

If we turn back to the three sample readings above, the Way of the Points can be used to learn more about the deeper factors at work in each one. In the first example, Diagram 4-1, the Way of the Points cannot be formed; the Judge, Conjunctio, has two points in its Fire line, while both of the Witnesses have one. This means that there is no particular meaning or driving force behind the accident in the store. It happened, it's over with, and now it's time to move on.

In the second example, Diagram 4-2, the Way of the Points can be formed. Carcer, the Judge, has one point as its Fire line; so does the Right Witness, Puella; so does the Second Niece, Puer, and so does the Third Mother, Cauda Draconis. This last figure is perhaps the most difficult of the sixteen, and represents losses, endings, and disruptions. It's possible, therefore, that what is behind the querent's desire to drop out of his degree program is simple depression, sparked by a loss or some other painful event in another area of his life. He should explore this possibility, get help if he needs it, and try to resolve the underlying issue before he makes a decision he may regret later on.

In the third example, Diagram 4-3, the Way of the Points can be formed but branches widely, including both Witnesses, all four Nieces and the Third and Fourth Mothers. These last two figures are the most important factors, but the First, Third, and Fourth Nieces are also ends of the Way of the Points and may be considered in the interpretation. The Mothers suggest that an important factor in the querent's success is a willingness to balance her passion for her art (Rubeus, the Fourth Mother) with the practical concerns of the business side of art (Acquisitio, the Third Mother). Caput Draconis, which appears twice as the First and Third Niece, suggests that her position as an artist just beginning her career may also stand in her favor.

The four triplicities

Another basic approach to geomantic interpretation makes use of four triplicities, or sets of three figures, drawn from the first twelve figures in the chart. These are often used in general readings done to tell the querent what broad patterns are at work in his or her life; they can also be used together with the Witnesses and Judge to relate some more specific question to the broader picture of the querent's life. They serve as an intermediate step between the methods we've already covered and the twelve houses, where most of the higher reaches of geomantic divination have their basis.

Each of the Four Nieces, together with the two Mothers or Daughters that produce it, makes up one of the triplicities, as shown in Diagram 4-4. The triplicities, their figures, and their meanings are as follows:

The first triplicity is made up of the First and Second Mother and the First Niece. It stands for the querent, including his or her circumstances, health, habits, and outlook on life.

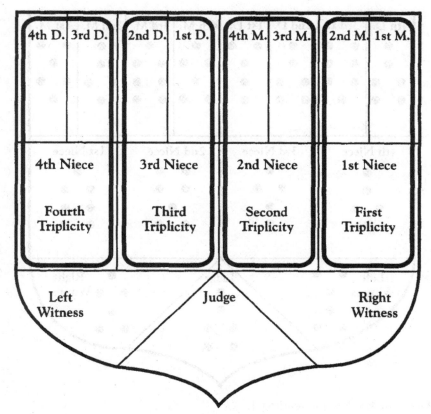

Diagram 4-4. The four triplicities.

The second triplicity is made up of the Third and Fourth Mothers and the Second Niece. It stands for the events shaping the querent's life at the time of the reading.

The third triplicity is made up of the First and Second Daughters and the Third Niece. It stands for the querent's home and work environment, the places he or she frequents, and the kinds of people who are found there. Family members and housemates are usually found in this triplicity.

The fourth triplicity is made up of the Third and Fourth Daughters and the Fourth Niece. It stands for the querent's friends and associates, and can also represent the people in authority over the querent.

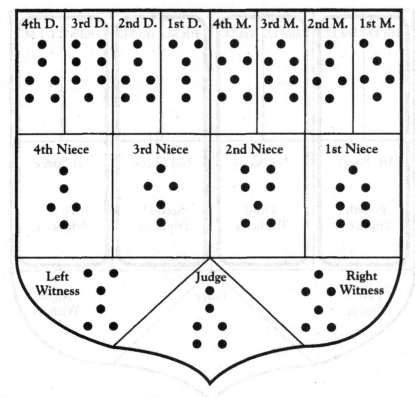

Diagram 4-5. Sample reading 4.

In each of these triplicities, the meanings of the three figures are combined to produce the meaning of the whole triplicity. The following sample reading, shown in Diagram 4-5, shows how this method of interpretation can work out in practice.

Sample reading 4

Here the querent is dissatisfied with the way his life is going at present, and asks how he should approach making changes. The first triplicity—Acquisitio, Puer, and Laetitia—describes him as passionate, forceful, energetic, and generally successful in life. He is likely to rush into things without looking first, but tends to get out of the scrapes this produces by a combination of energy and sheer luck (often a meaning of Laetitia).

The second triplicity—Laetitia, Amissio, and Albus—has to do with the current influences at work in his life. Here a significant loss is involved; but his luck has not deserted him, and the combination of Laetitia and Albus suggests that financially he is in good shape, though the impact of the loss is still an important factor.

The third triplicity—Caput Draconis, Fortuna Minor, and Puella—relates to the places where he spends time and the people with whom he associates there. Here there has been a change in the recent past, quite possibly related to a new love interest; Puella can often mean this in readings for heterosexual men or lesbians. (Likewise, Puer can have the same significance in readings for heterosexual women or gay men.) The presence of Fortuna Minor, though, suggests that this new beginning may take a certain amount of effort on his part; it will not come naturally, although it may happen with a good deal of speed.

The fourth triplicity—Tristitia, Fortuna Minor, and Puer—has to do with the querent's friends and associates, and here the presence of loss and change again plays a role. There is a good deal of energy and possibility in this aspect of his life, but Tristitia suggests that there may also be a quality of "stuckness" involved; perhaps the querent and his friends are caught up in a set of quarrels and unsatisfactory interactions that repeat like a broken record. The presence of Fortuna Minor suggests, though, that this can be changed, and it adds to the very active and transitional quality of the whole reading.

It's in this light that the Witnesses and Judge can be interpreted most clearly. The Right Witness is Amissio, the Left Witness Conjunctio, and the Judge Fortuna Minor, suggesting that the same process of rapid change that appears elsewhere in the reading is the keynote of his life at the present time. He is moving away from a significant loss and has not yet reached the point where his life starts coming back together. He needs to give the process the time it needs, to be willing to act suddenly when the circumstances favor it, and to pursue new possibilities as they open for him.

The twelve houses

The information given by the methods already covered—the interpretation of the Witnesses and Judge, the Way of the Points, and the four triplicities—is often enough to provide a clear response to the question. If it's useful to get a more detailed view of the situation, or to see how specific issues are affected by the pattern of forces at work in the reading, the focus of interpretation shifts, and the second of the traditional geomantic charts, the house chart, is used. In this new context, the figures are read not according to their heredity in the chart but in terms of their placement in the twelve geomantic houses.

These twelve houses, like the twelve houses of astrology on which they are modeled, serve to map out the parts of human life that are affected by one or another combination of forces in the reading. The twelve geomantic houses have slightly different meanings from their astrological equivalents, though. The following list of house rulerships, from medieval and Renaissance handbooks of geomancy, can be used as a general guide.

First houses: the querent, or the person for whom the divination is performed.

Second house: goods, material wealth, gain, business transactions, material things the querent desires, and stolen property.

Third house: brothers and sisters, the querent's neighbors and environment, short journeys, letters, advice, news and rumors.

Fourth house: father and mother, inheritances from parents, land, agriculture, buildings, construction, treasures, anything underground, ancient places and things, old age, hidden things, and the end of any matter.

Fifth house: pregnancy, children, entertainments and feasts, bodies of water, and rain.

Sixth house: servants, employees, small animals, illness, and injuries.

Seventh house: the querent's spouse or lover, love relationships, marriage, partnerships, quarrels, any unidentified person.

Eighth house: suffering, death, dangers, inheritances (other than from parents).

Ninth house: religion, philosophy, learning and education, the arts, wisdom, long journeys, divination.

Tenth house: employment, position in society, people in positions of authority, courts and judges, and the weather.

Eleventh house: friends, sources of help, good fortune, the querent's hopes and wishes.

Twelfth house: enemies, suffering, difficulties, any secret matter, imprisonment, large animals, the querent's fears.

Some modern systems of geomancy have complicated ways of assigning the figures of a geomantic chart to these twelve houses, but the traditional method is simplicity itself. The first twelve figures of the chart—the Mothers, Daughters, and Nieces—are simply put into the twelve houses in order. The First Mother thus becomes the figure

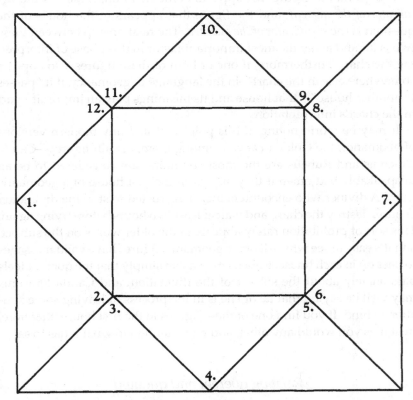

Diagram 4-6. The twelve geomantic houses.

in the first house, the Second Mother the figure in the second house, and so on, until the Fourth and final Niece is placed in the twelfth house.

The geomantic houses follow a subtle but definite logic, and it's a useful exercise to try putting different questions into their proper place in the system until you can identify the house that goes with any given question. In this phase of reading a geomantic chart, that skill is central to accurate interpretation. The querent (the person for whom the divination is done) and the subject of the divination (called the *quesited*) are each assigned to one of the twelve houses. The querent, as shown above, is always assigned to the first house, but the quesited, depending on its nature, may be found in any of the others.

The geomantic figure that appears in the first house, then, is the *significator of the querent*, and the figure that appears in the house of the quesited is the *significator of the quesited*. The relationship between these two is far and away the most important factor in this phase of interpreting the chart. Furthermore, if one or both of these figures also appears somewhere else in the chart—in the language of geomancy, if it "passes to another house"—that house and its meanings play an important part in the chart's interpretation.

It may be worth noting at this point that in many modern versions of geomancy, the Golden Dawn's among them, certain figures—Cauda Draconis and Rubeus are the most common—are considered to be an unspeakably bad omen if they appear in the first house of a geomantic chart. A diviner who encounters this is instructed to stop the divination at once, destroy the chart, and wait at least two hours before trying again. This sort of prohibition rarely appears in the older works on the subject, and it's easy to see why. All of the geomantic figures have valid messages to pass on in each house; Rubeus may mean simply that the querent feels passionately about the subject of the divination, and Cauda Draconis may well be saying that he or she is in the process of leaving some situation behind. If you find one of these figures in the first house, therefore, treat it as you would any other, and pay attention to what it has to say.

Relating querent and quesited

The old handbooks of geomancy give special names to the most important relationships that can occur between the two significators:

Occupation

The simplest of these, occupation, is where the same geomantic figure appears in the house of the querent and that of the quesited, as shown in Diagram 4-7.

The querent sent in an application to a prestigious university, and wants to know her chances of being accepted. The question, since it has

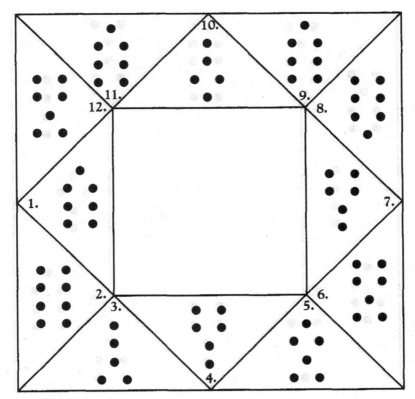

Diagram 4-7. Occupation.

to do with education, is a ninth house matter, and Laetitia appears in both the first and ninth houses. In any question that can be answered by a "yes" or "no," occupation means "yes," pure and simple; it is the strongest positive indication in geomancy. If (as here) the houses of querent and quesited are occupied by a favorable figure, this suggests that the querent will be happy with the result; if they are occupied by an unfavorable figure, the querent will get what he or she wants, but is likely to regret it later.

Conjunction

Nearly as positive an indicator as occupation is conjunction, when one of the significators passes to a house next to the house of the other significator, as in Diagram 4-8.

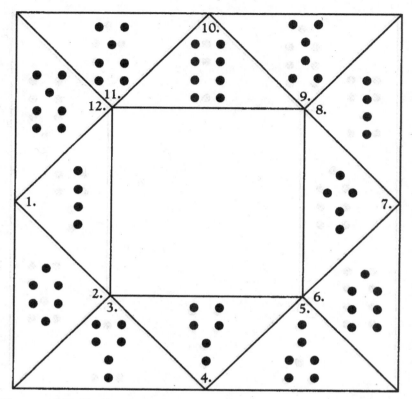

Diagram 4-8. Conjunction.

Here the querent has quarreled with his lover and wants to know if there is hope for a reconciliation. The figure in the first house, the house of the querent, is Via, and that in the seventh house, the house of the querent's lover, is Puella. Via also appears in the eighth house, in conjunction with Puella in the seventh, and this suggests that a reconciliation is possible. Traditional lore has it that when the querent's significator passes to a conjunction with that of the quesited, as happens here, the querent will achieve what he or she wants, but will have to work for it. When the significator of the quesited passes into a conjunction with that of the querent, on the other hand, no effort by the querent is needed. Here, this rule would suggest that the querent should be willing to make the first move toward a reconciliation.

As always, the meanings of the figures themselves need to be included in the interpretation. Here, in particular, the role of Via is very important. Via always implies change. As the significator of the querent, it suggests that he may have a certain amount of growing and changing to do if the reconciliation is to work!

Mutation

Another positive indicator is mutation, where the significators of the querent and the quesited both pass to neighboring houses elsewhere in the chart, as in Diagram 4-9.

Here the querent is unhappy with her present employment and hopes to find a better position somewhere else. Her significator is Fortuna Minor, which is a good sign to start with, as this figure's meanings include "protection going out." The significator of the quesited,

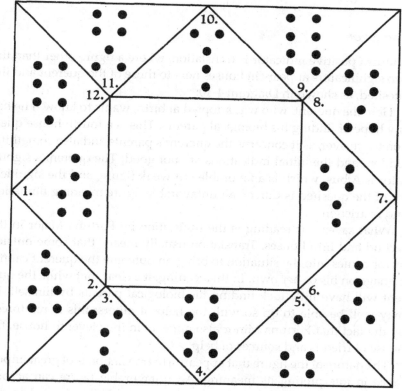

Diagram 4-9. Mutation.

since employment is a tenth house matter, is Caput Draconis, another positive figure, but without a link between the significators this might represent a good job that remains out of reach.

The link is provided, however, by the mutation between Fortuna Minor in the second house and Caput Draconis in the third. Mutation typically implies that the goal the querent has in mind needs to be sought along unexpected paths, and the house where the significator of the quesited occurs is often a guide to where those paths are to be found. Here the significator of the quesited passes to the third house, which represents the querent's siblings, neighbors, and nearby environment, and the same figure also appears in the eleventh house of friends and sources of help. This suggests that she would be well advised to talk to friends and neighbors about her job search and to follow up openings in her own neighborhood rather than putting all her efforts into job agencies or the classified ads.

Translation

A fourth positive indicator is translation, where a figure other than the two significators appears in houses next to those of the querent and the quesited, as shown in Diagram 4-10.

Here the querent, who was adopted at birth, wants to know if he has any hope of finding his biological parents. This is a fourth house question twice over, as it concerns the querent's parents and also something hidden, and the initial indications are not good. The querent's significator is Albus, which is a favorable but weak figure, and the significator of the quesited is Carcer, an unfavorable figure meaning limitation and restriction.

What saves this reading is the translation by Fortuna Major in the second and fifth houses. Translation usually means that some outside factor comes into the situation to bring an outcome the querent cannot manage on his or her own. In this reading, it's clear that while the querent will have little luck finding his biological parents by himself, he may well be able to do so with the help of others; this is reinforced by the fact that Fortuna Minor also appears in the eleventh house, the house of friends and sources of help.

The nature of the figure that appears in a translation is of great importance in interpreting its meaning. An unfavorable figure can accomplish a translation just as effectively as a favorable one, but when this

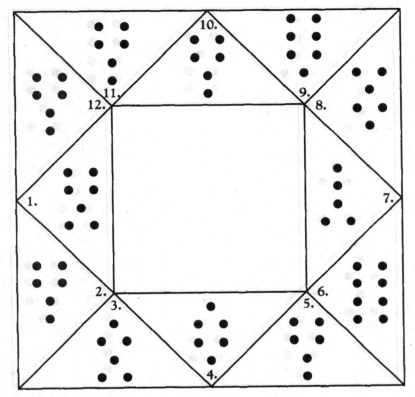

Diagram 4-10. Translation.

happens it often means that the situation will involve some unpleas-
ant experiences before it's resolved. A weak figure such as Albus or
Populus, when it carries out a translation, often means that the matter is
brought to a conclusion by some unlikely means, or even by what looks
like pure coincidence. If the figure that accomplishes the translation
represents a person, as it often does, it's possible to get some idea of
that person's appearance from the figure.

Lack of relationship

The chief negative indicator in interpreting a geomantic reading
through the twelve houses is a lack of relationship between the significators of the querent and the quesited, as shown in Diagram 4-11.

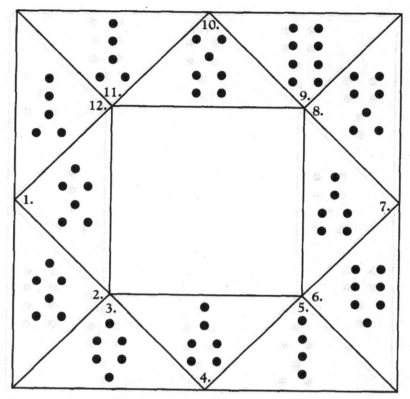

Diagram 4-11. Lack of relationship.

The querent and her partner have been trying for some time to have a child, without success, and she wants to know what their chances are of doing so at all. Pregnancy and children are fifth house matters; the querent's significator is Amissio, not a good omen, and that of the quesited is Via, which is an unfavorable figure in many contexts. The critical factor, though, is that there is no direct connection of any kind between these figures. Amissio appears in one other place in the chart, the second house; Via appears nowhere else but the fifth; there is no third figure that interacts with these two and brings the matter to a successful conclusion. Barring favorable Witnesses and Judge (which do not occur here: the Witnesses are Rubeus and Cauda Draconis, and the Judge Amissio again), a chart like this can offer little hope.

Aspect

A more subtle category of interaction, which can have either favorable or unfavorable meanings, may be found in aspects between the significators. Aspects, like houses, were brought into geomancy from astrological sources, and had to be modified in certain ways to fit the different nature of geomantic divination.

The most important of these modifications is that aspects aren't read between the houses of the querent and the quesited. This is a function of the fixed meanings of the different houses. The first house is always in a trine aspect, which is favorable, with the fifth and ninth houses, and in a square aspect, which is unfavorable, with the fourth and tenth; to read these aspects as meaningful would imply, for example, that questions involving children would always get a favorable answer, while questions involving employment would always get an unfavorable one! For this reason, aspects between the significators must involve at least one of them passing to a different house.

There are four aspects which are used in geomancy, besides conjunction (which we've already examined): sextile, square, trine, and opposition.

The **sextile** aspect in astrology occurs when two planets are at a 60-degree angle to each other. In geomancy, two figures are sextile when there is one house between them. This aspect is favorable.

The **square** aspect in astrology takes place when two planets are at a 90-degree angle to each other. In geomancy, two figures are square when there are two houses between them. This aspect is unfavorable.

The **trine** aspect in astrology occurs when two planets are at a 120-degree angle to each other. In geomancy, two figures are trine when there are three houses between them. This aspect is favorable.

Opposition in astrology takes place when two planets are at a 180-degree angle to each other, on opposite sides of the sky. In geomancy, two figures are in opposition when there are five houses between them— when, in other words, they are in opposite houses in the chart. This aspect is unfavorable.

When one of the significators passes to another house and comes into an aspect with the other, this provides a favorable or unfavorable sign, depending on whether the aspect itself is favorable or unfavorable.

If the significators are also linked by occupation, conjunction, mutation, or translation, a favorable aspect will add to the positive nature of the reading; this occurs in Diagram 4-9, where the mutation between the significators in the second and third houses is reinforced by a sextile between Fortuna Minor in the fifth house and Caput Draconis in the third. Caput Draconis in the tenth house springs to the third and eleventh houses, and both of these are sextile to the first house. (The apparent square between the tenth and first house doesn't count; remember that aspects aren't read between the significators in their own houses!) Favorable aspects themselves count as connections between the significators, and a sextile or trine with no unfavorable aspects contradicting it is a clear positive answer.

If the significators are connected by one of the major relationships, but there is also an unfavorable aspect linking them, the result is still favorable, but there will be trouble involved. When an unfavorable aspect is the only connection between the significators, though, the answer is negative. This is the case in Diagram 4-11, where Amissio passes to the second house, in square aspect with Via in the fifth.

Whenever an aspect is involved, it can be read as a specific source of help or hindrance in the situation. In Diagram 4-9, for instance, the sextile aspect reinforces the suggestion that the querent should seek help from friends and neighbors in her job search. In Diagram 4-11, on the other hand, the fact that Amissio passes to the second house, into an unfavorable aspect, suggests that the childless couple may not have the resources to afford the very expensive modern medical treatments for infertility—or simply that money spent on these would be wasted.

Reconciling the judge and the houses

Under certain circumstances, the indications of the Judge and Witnesses will seem to contradict those provided by the significators and their relationship. When this occurs, there are two methods of putting both sets of messages into a common context and making sense of the apparent disagreement. The first is made by combining the significators, and the second is made by combining the querent's significator with the Judge.

Combining the significators

First of all, one can combine the significators to produce a new figure using the same additive process that generates the Nieces, Witnesses, and Judge. When this is used, the figure that is generated out of the two significators represents a tightly focused view of the way that querent and quesited interact. This can be seen in Diagram 4-12.

Here the querent is considering an investment for money she has set aside for her retirement. Money matters are assigned to the second

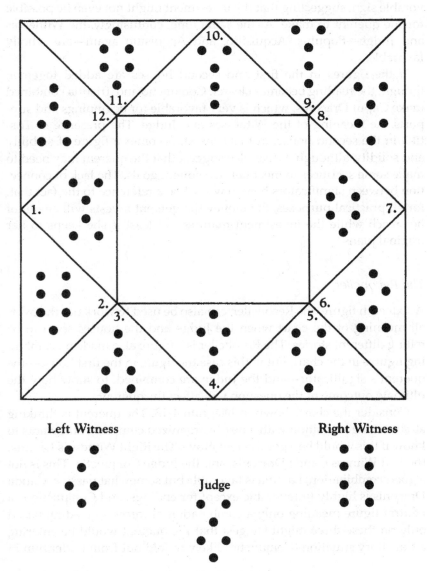

Left Witness

Right Witness

Judge

Diagram 4-12. Reconciling the Judge and the houses.

house, and the figure in the second house in this reading is Tristitia, which is an ambiguous omen, as it can mean stability (the querent's primary goal in this investment) as well as suffering. Tristitia and Conjunctio, the figure in the first house, do not pass to any other house or come into any interaction at all; normally this would be a sharply unfavorable sign, suggesting that the investment might not even be possible for the querent to make. At the same time, confusingly, the Witnesses and Judge—Populus, Acquisitio, and Acquisitio again—are wholly favorable.

If the figures in the first and second houses are added together, though, the reading becomes clearer. Conjunctio and Tristitia combined make Caput Draconis, which is very favorable for beginnings and supports the meaning of the Witnesses and Judge. The presence of Tristitia in the second house, in this context, becomes a figure of stability and solidity, although it does also suggest that the querent may need to make some sacrifices to meet her investment goals. The lack of connection between significators here may well be a reference to the fact that, for all practical purposes, the money the querent invests will be out of her reach while the investment matures—at least if she keeps to her original plans.

The Reconciler

A sixteenth figure, the Reconciler, can also be used to work out the overall meaning of the chart when the Judge and the houses seem to be telling different stories. The Reconciler is a figure also made by combining figures in the chart, but in this case the figure in the first house—the querent's significator—and the Judge are combined, to show how the ultimate outcome of the question will affect the querent.

Consider the chart shown in Diagram 4-13. The querent is thinking about taking a position with a newly organized company, and wants to know if this would be a good career move. The Right Witness is Laetitia, the Left Witness Cauda Draconis, and the Judge Conjunctio. This is not a good combination; Laetitia is favorable but somewhat passive, Cauda Draconis is highly unfavorable except for endings, and Conjunctio is a neutral figure meaning only a combination of forces. A reading based only on these three might suggest that the querent would be entering a transitory situation (Conjunctio) likely to fold out from under him in

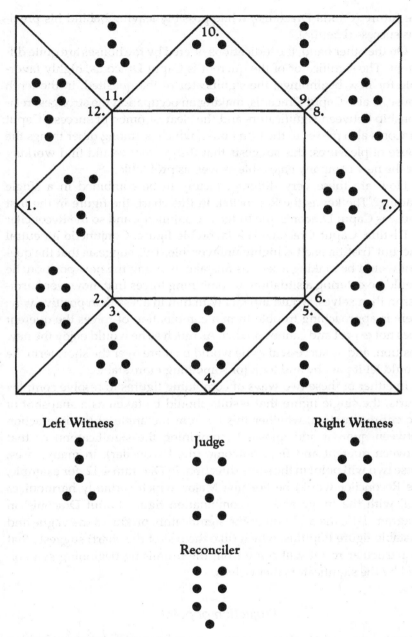

Diagram 4-13. The Reconciler.

the future (Cauda Draconis), while possibly leaving behind his previous success (Laetitia).

On the other hand, the indications offered by the houses are quite different. The significator of the querent is Caput Draconis, highly favorable for new beginnings; the significator of the quesited, in the tenth house, is also Caput Draconis, making an occupation the strongest relationship between significators and the clearest omen of success. Caput Draconis also passes to the fifth house, which is among other things the house of pleasures; this suggests that the querent would find working for the new company enjoyable as well as profitable.

How are these very different factors to be combined in a single reading? The key is the Reconciler. In this chart, the figure in the first house is Caput Draconis, the Judge is Conjunctio, and so the Reconciler is Tristitia. Caput Draconis is a favorable figure, Conjunctio a neutral one, but Tristitia itself is highly unfavorable. This suggests that the querent would be making a serious mistake in taking the new position; he would be entering a situation of combining forces that, however harmless in themselves, would interact with him in a less than positive way; there is approaching trouble from a combination of forces the querent does not expect and cannot predict. As much as he would enjoy the new position, and as successful as he would be there over the short term, he should let it pass by and look for something more stable.

In either of these two ways of combining figures to resolve complex charts, the single figure that results should be taken as a snapshot of the entire situation, whether this be from the angle of the interaction between querent and quesited (combining the significators) or that between querent and final outcome (the Reconciler). In many cases, these two will point in the same direction. In Diagram 4-12, for example, the Reconciler would be Fortuna Major, which certainly harmonizes well with the Judge and the combination figure Caput Draconis; in Diagram 4-13, the addition of the significators produces the vague and unstable figure Populus, which (like the rest of the chart) suggests that no particular result will come from the promising beginning symbolized by the significators themselves.

Projection of points

A special method of interpretation that can be used to ferret out hidden factors in the chart makes use of the Projection of Points. This is calculated by counting the number of single points in the first twelve figures of the chart, leaving the double points uncounted. Take the total number of single points and subtract 12; if the result is more than 12, subtract 12 again, and repeat until you have a number less than 12. This gives the number of the house that represents the hidden factor in the situation. (If the final number is 0, this stands for the twelfth house.)

In Diagram 4-13, for example, there are a total of 30 single points in the first twelve figures. Twelve can be subtracted from 30 twice— 30–12 = 18, 18–12 = 6—and so 6, the remainder, is the number of the house that contains the hidden factor in the reading. The sixth house is the house of illness, and the figure in this position in Diagram 4-13 is Amissio; this suggests that the new position might cause the querent to suffer a work-related illness, with the possibility of permanent damage to his health.

The company of houses

Another help in interpreting a geomantic chart is to consider the Company of Houses, a specific pattern of relationship between pairs of houses in the chart. In this pattern, the first and second houses are always paired, as are the third and fourth, the fifth and sixth, and so on, around the chart. It's important to keep this in mind, as one of the more common mistakes in this phase of interpretation is to read the Company between houses that aren't paired—for instance, between the second and third house, or the tenth and eleventh.

The first step in using this method is to examine the house paired with the house of each of the significators, to see whether company exists between one or both of the significators and the figures in the paired houses. There are four ways in which company can exist: company simple, company demi-simple, company compound, and a fourth that has no traditional name.

Company simple exists when the two paired houses share the same figure—for example, in Diagram 4-12, where Caput Draconis appears in both the ninth and tenth houses.

Company demi-simple exists when two paired houses are occupied by figures ruled by the same planet—for example, if Albus appeared in the third house and Conjunctio in the fourth, both these figures being ruled by Mercury.

Company compound exists when two paired houses are occupied by opposite figures; the oppositions between figures are shown in Table 4-1.

Table 4-1. Opposite figures.

Puer	is opposite to	Puella
Amissio	is opposite to	Acquisitio
Albus	is opposite to	Rubeus
Populus	is opposite to	Via
Fortuna Major	is opposite to	Fortuna Minor
Conjunctio	is opposite to	Carcer
Tristitia	is opposite to	Laetitia
Caput Draconis	is opposite to	Cauda Draconis

The last form of company exists when the figures in the paired houses have the same first line. For example, in Diagram 4-8, Puella in the seventh house and Via in the eighth house are in company since each has a single point in its first line. By contrast, in Diagram 4-7, Cauda Draconis in the third house is not in company with Fortuna Major in the fourth since they have different first lines.

When company exists between a significator and the figure in its paired house, two conclusions can be drawn from it. First, the figure in company with the significator can be used to tell something about the role of friends, family, or associates in whatever the significator governs. The company of the querent gives information about the querent's own associates, while the company of the quesited offers insight into the people associated with whoever or whatever the quesited happens to be. If there is no company for either or both, on the other hand, this can be taken as a sign that other people are not deeply involved in this phase of the matter.

Additionally, there is an element of time in the relationship between figures in company. The odd-numbered house is said to show the present, while the even-numbered house paired with it shows the future. This is read as though both figures were in the significator's house; the meaning usually given to the paired house does not come into play.

Thus if the significator of the quesited is in the fourth house, and is in company with a figure in the third, the third house meanings of communication, short journeys, and so on do not influence the companion's role unless the companion has some other function in the reading—for example, if it plays a part in a mutation or a translation.

In all cases where company of figures exists, it's often useful to combine the two figures that are in company and use the resulting figure to show the effect that the relationship between companions has on the whole question.

If nothing makes sense

The old manuals, finally, have two last-ditch methods to use if the chart you get makes no sense, however you work with it. Both of these depend on the same process of combining two figures to make a third that is used so often in the more advanced interpretive methods of geomancy.

The first of these methods involves adding together the figures in the first and fourth houses of the chart to produce a new Right Witness, and then those in the seventh and tenth houses to produce a new Left Witness. Once this is done, the two new Witnesses are added together to make a new Judge, and the reading is interpreted as though these were the original Witnesses and Judge.

The second method is used only when this first method produces no clear result. In this method, the figures in the first and fifth houses are added together to make a new First Mother, those in the second and sixth to create a new Second Mother, those in the third and seventh give rise to a new Third Mother, and those in the fourth and eighth produce a new Fourth Mother. Once these have been generated, the entire process of laying out the chart is done over again using these secondary Mothers, producing Daughters, Nieces, Witnesses, and a Judge, as before.

Particular questions

A good deal of space in medieval and Renaissance manuals of geomancy went into specific methods for answering particular types of questions. Some of the material in this branch of geomantic lore is of little value at the present time—few modern geomancers will ever need to divine the best way to attack an enemy castle, for instance—but since human needs and goals change very little over the centuries, a good many of these questions are still commonly asked today. The following section deals with some of the most common of these.

Identifying unknown persons

The seventh house governs any unidentified person, and the physical description corresponding to the figure in that house can be used as a guide to the appearance of the person in question. If the figure in this house is in company with the figure in the eighth, this figure can be used to supplement the description, although the seventh-house figure takes precedence.

In a chart cast to identify someone unknown, any house to which the significator of the quesited passes can be read as information about the unknown person. If the figure in the seventh house passes to the tenth, for example, the unknown person is in a position of authority; if it passes to the fifth, the unknown person is likely to be a child; if it passes to the eleventh, the unknown person may be a friend of the querent, and so on.

For example, the querent in Diagram 4-14 has had a piece of heirloom jewelry stolen, apparently by a visitor to her apartment, and hopes to identify and confront the thief directly rather than taking the matter to the police. The figure in the seventh house, Rubeus, represents a muscular redhead or reddish brunette with a deep voice and red spots or blotches on the face. Rubeus also passes to the eleventh house, indicating that the thief is probably a friend of the querent's. It should be noted that the eleventh house is in sextile aspect to the querent's significator; this suggests that the querent may well be able to resolve the problem and regain the piece of jewelry by talking to the thief and appealing to his or her better nature.

Locating persons

If the querent wishes to locate a person, the divination can be treated as an ordinary seventh house question if the person is not otherwise related to the querent, or is the querent's spouse or partner. Other relationships between the querent and the person to be located require other houses; parents are in the fourth house, children in the fifth, friends in the eleventh, and enemies in the twelfth. In any of these cases, the relationship

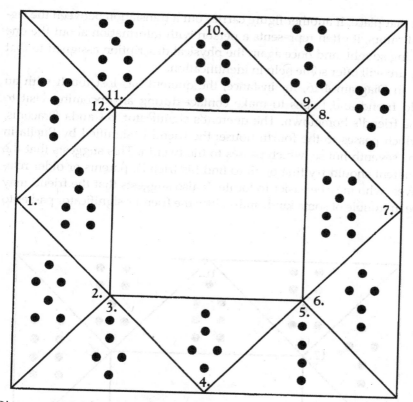

Diagram 4-14. Identifying unknown persons.

(or lack of it) between the querent's significator and that of the quesited will predict whether the querent will be successful in his or her search.

If the significator of the quesited passes to any other house in the chart, the nature of the house offers a clue to where the person can be found. If the figure passes to the fourth house, for example, the person may be in a rural location, a garden, or some underground place; if it passes to the sixth, the person may be in a hospital; if it passes to the twelfth, he or she may be in jail; if it passes to the eighth, the person sought may be dead.

Similarly, if the querent's significator passes to any other place in the chart, this suggests a place he or she should look; while it is unlikely that the person being sought will turn up there, it's much more likely that the querent will learn something of the person's whereabouts in that place. If another figure carries out a translation between the significators, it often represents a person with information about the one being sought, and once again the physical description assigned to that figure will offer some help in identification.

In Diagram 4-15, for instance, the querent has lost touch with an old friend and hopes to make contact during an upcoming visit to the friend's hometown. The querent's significator is Cauda Draconis, which passes to the fourth house; the friend is signified by Puella in the seventh house, which passes to the twelfth. This suggests that the querent should try first of all to find his friend's parents or older relatives, who may be easier to locate. It also suggests that the friend may be in trouble of some kind, and—since the friend's significator passes to

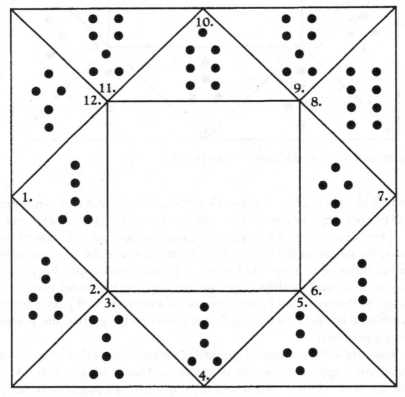

Diagram 4-15. Locating persons.

a conjunction with the querent's—that the friend may actually be trying to contact the querent, or may do so soon.

Recovering lost objects

This seems to have been a very common reason for geomantic divination in the Middle Ages, and there are a number of different ways to approach it. First, and simplest, it can be treated as any other question, with the figure in the fourth house as the significator of the quesited. The relationship (or lack of it) between the significators then determines whether the lost thing will be recovered or not, and the figure in the fourth house offers information about the place where it is—for example, Carcer might suggest that it is in a safe or a locked room, Via suggests a road or street, and so on. It is also possible, and traditional, to ask whether the object has been lost in a specific place, and to continue casting charts until the answer is positive and a search can be mounted.

There are also more specialized methods. One involves the distinction between stable and mobile figures (refer to Quality in figure descriptions, chapter 2). Using this method, if a stable figure appears in the fourth house, the object will be found; if a mobile one, the object is gone for good. In either case, the location where it was lost can be determined by seeing if the figure passes to another house in the chart, just as with unknown persons. If the figure passes to the first house, the object was lost wherever the querent spends most of his or her time; if it passes to the seventh, it was lost in a place associated with the querent's lover, spouse, or business partner; if it passes to the eleventh, it was lost some place where large numbers of people gather, and so on. If the figure appears only in the fourth house, the object was lost somewhere at home.

In Diagram 4-16, for example, an important packet of papers has been misplaced, and the querent wants to know whether they can be recovered and, if so, where and how. The querent's significator is Amissio, appropriately enough, which passes to the third house; the significator of the quesited is Puella, which passes to the seventh. There is a conjunction between the two significators, and Puella is a stable figure, so both these factors suggest that the papers can indeed be recovered. The movement of Puella to the seventh suggests that they are presently at the home of the querent's lover, and the movement of Amissio to the

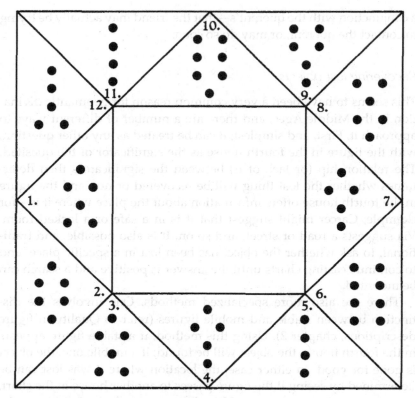

Diagram 4-16. Recovering lost objects.

third (into trine with the seventh) points to the best strategy: since the third house governs short journeys, he should go there himself and help search for the papers.

It's also possible to work out the location of the lost object by a set of directional correspondences. The outer elements of the figures are the key to this system: figures of Air correspond to the east, those of Fire correspond to the south, those of Water to the west, and those of Earth to the north. The figure that appears in the fourth house, depending on its outer element, gives the direction in which the querent needs to search for the object. If the querent already knows the general area where the lost object is, by a previous divination or by some other means, a chart can be cast to find out whether the object is in the northern, southern, western, or eastern quarter of the area, and (if the area is very large) this can be repeated to narrow down the area to one that can be searched effectively with the resources the querent has available.

Discovering the date or time of a predicted event

A chart should be cast specially for this purpose. If you need to know the part of the year in which the event will happen, find the house that corresponds to the event; the astrological sign attributed to the figure in that house is the sign the Sun will be in when the event happens. (Any astrological almanac or, for that matter, any newspaper astrology column will give the dates of the Sun's passage through each sign.) The figures Caput Draconis and Cauda Draconis, which do not correspond to signs, indicate that the date cannot be predicted; Caput Draconis tends to mean that it's too early to tell, Cauda Draconis that the event will never happen.

If you know the month or sign and need to know the exact day, cast a new chart and consider the figure in the house governing the predicted event. If that figure does not pass to any other house in the chart, the event will happen in the first week of the month. If it passes to the next house, the event will happen in the second week; to the house after that, in the third week; to the one after that (the fourth in all, counting the original house as first), in the fourth week. The cycle then begins over again. The whole pattern is shown in Diagram 4-17, choosing for examples an event of the seventh house—a wedding, perhaps—and one of the tenth house—say, being promoted to a position of authority. Remember that the pattern always begins counting from the house governing the event.

Once the week has been determined, the day can be discovered by checking the planetary correspondence of the sign in the house governing the event. The link between days and planets follows the traditional names of the days of the week themselves as noted in Table 4-2.

Sample reading 5

In Diagram 4-18, for example, the querent is expecting an important letter and wants to know when it will arrive. In this case she already knows the approximate month—either by a previous divination or by way of other sources of information—and simply needs to know the day and week. Letters are a third house matter, and the figure in the third house is Conjunctio, which also appears in the first house. Counting around the chart from the third house, the first house represents the third week of the month; Conjunctio is ruled by Mercury, and so the letter will arrive on the third Wednesday of the month.

Determining whether a dream is significant

In the Middle Ages, dreams were recognized as a potential source of information and insight about past, present, and future events; "a dream that is not interpreted," ran a proverb of the time, "is like a letter that

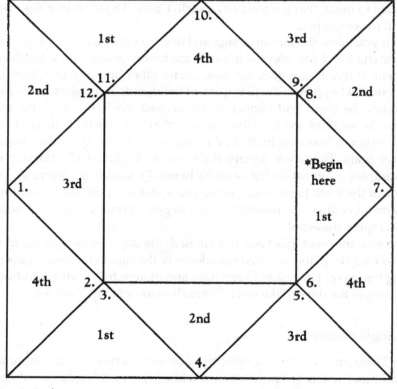

(Continued)

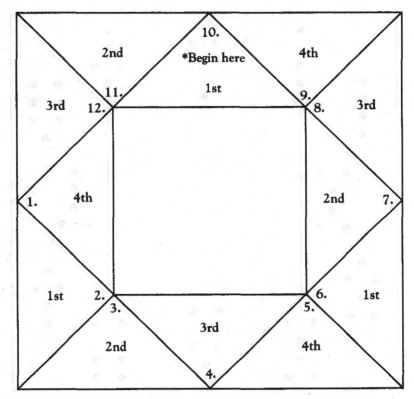

Diagram 4-17. Time patterns for a tenth house question.

Table 4-2. The planets and days of the week.

Sun	Sunday
Moon	Monday
Mars (in the old English pantheon, Tiw)	Tuesday
Mercury (or Woden)	Wednesday
Jupiter (or Thor)	Thursday
Venus (or Freya)	Friday
Saturn	Saturday

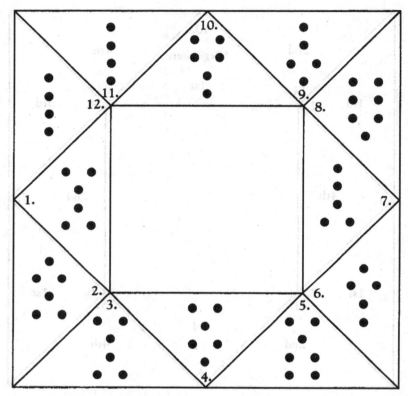

Diagram 4-18. Sample reading 5.

is not opened." At the same time, medieval dreamlore distinguished between significant dreams, which might have important messages to give, and meaningless ones, which were simply a reflection of stray moods and memories. Geomancy was among the methods used to sort out the two kinds.

Dreams correspond to the ninth house of the chart, and one simple way to check them is to cast a chart and check the figure in the ninth house; a stable figure suggests that the dream is significant, a mobile figure that it means nothing. If a stable figure in the ninth house passes to another house, this points toward the aspect of the querent's life to which the dream relates, and this can be a helpful clue. The question can also be treated as an ordinary ninth house question, and judged based on the relationship (or lack of it) between the significators.

Checking news and rumors

When geomancy was at its height, news was even more inaccurate than it is today, and checking the accuracy of rumors and reports from distant places was another very common reason for geomantic divination. Here again, the question can be cast and judged as an ordinary third house question; on the other hand, it was also traditional to simply cast a chart and check the figure in the third house. Stable figures suggest that the news or rumor is true, mobile ones that it is false. The figures Via and Populus have a special message in this application: both of them suggest that the information has become garbled in transmission and is neither wholly true nor completely false.

These approaches can also be combined, as in Diagram 4-19. Here the querent has received a phone call from a very upset friend, who has

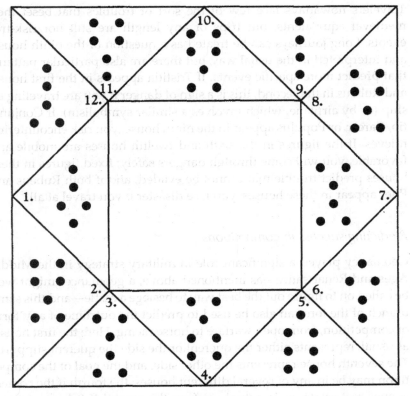

Diagram 4-19. Checking news and rumors.

heard that a third person, a mutual friend of both, has disappeared. The friend who made the call believes that the mutual friend may have committed suicide.

The chart, fortunately, says otherwise. Conjunctio in the third house, the significator of the quesited, is a moving figure, and thus suggests that the rumor is false; it passes to the seventh, into opposition with the querent's significator in the first, and this is the only interaction between the significators. The eighth house, the house of suffering and death, plays no role at all, and in fact it contains the benign figure Albus. Based on the movement of Conjunctio, it might even be worth suggesting that the mutual friend may have "disappeared" because he is spending most of his time with a new love interest!

Anticipating problems while traveling

Travelers nowadays face few of the sort of troubles that beset their medieval equivalents, but trips of any length are still not risk-free events. Long journeys can be treated as a question of the ninth house, and interpreted in the usual way, but there are also particular patterns that predict more specific events. If Tristitia appears in the first house, and Rubeus in the second, this is a sign of danger if you are traveling by ship (or by airplane, which involves a similar symbolism). If Conjunctio, Carcer, or Populus appear in the ninth house, you risk encountering thieves. If the figures in the sixth and twelfth houses are mobile and favorable, you will come through dangers safely; fixed figures in these houses predict trouble that cannot be evaded, and if both Rubeus and Puer appear in these houses, you face disaster if you travel at all.

Predicting success in competitions

Geomancy played a significant role in military strategy in the Middle Ages and Renaissance—as mentioned above, a geomancer might well be called on to figure out the best way to besiege a castle—and this same branch of the lore can also be used to predict the outcome of any form of competition, from open warfare to horse racing. Here the first house, as usual, represents either the querent or the side the querent supports. The seventh house represents the other side, and the goal of the competition may be in any of several different houses: the fourth if the contest is over real estate, as in actual warfare; the second if it is for money;

the tenth if it is for honor, fame, professional advancement, or the sheer fun of the sport.

In charts of this kind, it's necessary to pay attention to the relationships among all three houses involved. Generally speaking, if one side has a connection to the house of the goal and the other side does not, the first side will win. The same is the case if one side has a better connection than the other—for instance, if one is linked to the house of the goal by occupation, and the other by mutation, or if one has any of the major forms of connection while the other is linked to the goal only by aspects.

If the chart shows a relationship between the two contending sides, this can mean that the struggle results in a tie or is settled peacefully. An occupation linking the two sides often means that the contest results in an alliance or the growth of a friendship; a conjunction often means that the side whose significator passes into the conjunction seeks a settlement or a truce; a mutation often means that both sides decide to settle; a translation suggests that some third party will bring about a resolution. (In this case, check the aspects of the translating figure to the house governing the goal; if it has a solid link to the goal, and neither of the other significators do, this can mean that some other person or group will win the competition and leave both sides out of luck!) Finally, if there are no connections linking any of the three significators together, it's possible that the competition will end in a stalemate, or even that it will be called off because of some outside factor.

In Diagram 4-20, the querent has applied for a new management position at the company where she works. Several of her co-workers have also applied for the same opening, and she wants to know her chances of getting the position in the face of so much competition.

Her significator is Albus, in the first house; the other applicants can be lumped together in the seventh, and their significator is Fortuna Minor, while the goal is a tenth house matter and its significator is therefore Laetitia. Neither the querent's significator nor that of the other applicants passes anywhere in the chart; Laetitia, on the other hand, passes to the twelfth house, into conjunction with the querent's significator. It also passes to the fourth house, where it forms a square with both the querent and the other applicants. The querent will get the position, therefore, but there may be some trouble over the matter—perhaps hard feelings on the part of those who were passed over.

One additional aspect of the traditional lore worth mentioning here is a way to determine the best approach for any given competition.

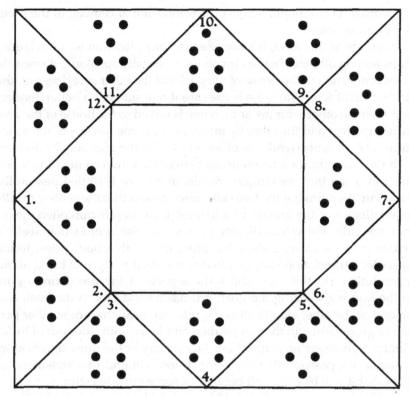

Diagram 4-20. Predicting success in competition.

This is based on the planetary symbolism of the figures, and depends on the figure in the first house.

The figures of Saturn (Carcer and Tristitia) suggest an approach based on persistence, patience, and endurance. The figures of Jupiter (Acquisitio and Laetitia) suggest relying on powerful friends, support networks, or financial resources. Those of Mars (Puer and Rubeus) suggest that the best approach is one of sheer brute force. Those of the Sun (Fortuna Major and Fortuna Minor) suggest that the querent's own personal qualities will be enough to carry the day. The figures of Venus (Amissio and Puella) suggest that tact, gentleness, and a willingness to negotiate will bring success. The figures of Mercury (Albus and Conjunctio) suggest an approach based on communication, strategic thinking, and possibly deception. The figures of the Moon (Populus and Via) suggest that success will come through responding deftly to the situation as it develops.

In the example given above, the querent's significator, Albus, suggests that she should concentrate on making the most of her communications abilities, and think through a plan of action intended to present her as a viable candidate for the new job. The significator of the other applicants, Fortuna Minor, hints that they may not be taking any active steps to pursue the position, and this may well be a major factor in the querent's success.

Predicting the weather

Even at present, with the full armament of modern computers, communications, and satellites to draw on, weather prediction is inexact at best, and divinatory methods such as geomancy may still not be completely without value! The lore of geomantic weather prediction has its roots in ancient and medieval traditions of meteorology far too complex and extensive to cover here, but there are some basic principles that can serve as a starting point for experiments.

One of the more important of these relies on the assignment of the figures to the four elements. In the traditional system, Fire is warm and dry, Water cold and wet, Air warm and wet, and Earth cold and dry. The tenth house of a geomantic chart governs weather, and so the simplest way of forecasting the weather is to cast a chart for the day in question and consider the inner element of the figure that appears in the tenth house. Tristitia, for example, is a figure of Earth and so means cold and dry weather, though "cold" will of course have a different meaning in July than it has in January, and differences in local climate conditions also have to be taken into account.

Another method of prediction makes use of the stable and mobile qualities of the figures. Here the question to be asked and answered is whether the weather on the day of the divination will change by some specified day or time; a mobile figure in the tenth house means yes, a stable one no, and in the former case the element and nature of the figure often has something to say about what the change may be.

Gardeners and farmers may also find it useful to ask, as their medieval and Renaissance equivalents did, if the weather in the upcoming season promises a good crop or a poor one. Here both the tenth house (governing the weather) and the fourth house (governing the soil) have

to be consulted. Figures of the elements Air and Water favor agriculture, while figures belonging to Fire and Earth are bad for crops; a fiery
figure often means too much heat or too little rain when it appears in
the tenth and indicates pest problems in the fourth, while an earthy
figure often means frosts and cool weather in the tenth and soil deficien-
cies in the fourth.

If the figures in both these houses favor planting, expect a good yield.
If one house has a favorable figure and the other an unfavorable one,
it's often possible to correct for the predicted problem and still get a
fair crop. If both houses have fiery or earthy figures, on the other hand,
the crop is likely to be poor, and there's probably not much you can do
about it.

Finding buried treasure

Most of the old textbooks of geomancy, finally, give guidelines for
locating buried treasure. Historically speaking, this has been quite a
common reason for divination and magic of all kinds, and for good
reason. In the days before modern banks evolved, secret burial was one
of the few relatively secure ways to store wealth, and the location of
such burials might easily be lost through an unexpected death or any
of the other confusions of a troubled age. Archeologists in Europe, it
may be noted, still turn up old caches of coins and precious metals now
and then. Few modern geomancers are likely to be so fortunate, but
for those interested in experimenting with the method, the following
guidelines may be of interest.

The location of buried treasure is a fourth house question, like anything else underground, and the usual connections between the significators should be considered. The figure in the fourth house, however,
has the most important role, as it says something about the nature and
condition of what is buried. Stable figures mean that the buried treasure
may still exist; mobile figures mean that nothing will be found. Favorable figures indicate that what is buried is something of value, while
unfavorable ones promise a worthless find.

Whether the figure in the fourth house passes to another house is
also important. A stable figure that does not pass to any other house
means that the treasure has not been moved since its burial; one that
goes to another house means that something was there once but that
it was removed to another place in the past, and it's often possible to

guess the place where it was taken by noting the house to which the figure passes.

In Diagram 4-21, for example, the querent has recalled an old story about a great-grandfather who went to the Yukon during the Gold Rush

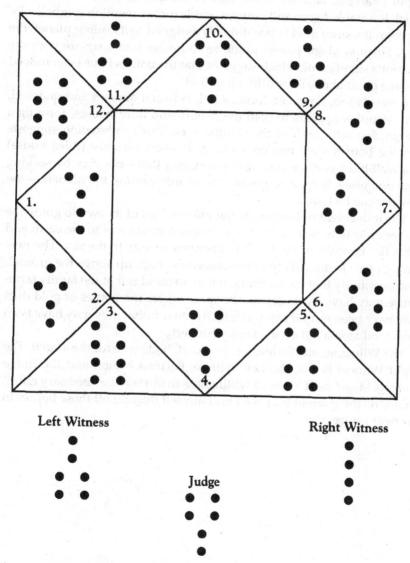

Diagram 4-21. Finding buried treasure.

days and, so it was said, buried old whiskey bottles full of gold dust on the family's property, where the querent now lives. The querent is understandably interested in finding these if they exist!

The chart suggests that he may have a chance. His significator is Caput Draconis, and the significator of the quesited is Fortuna Major, which is a stable figure and very favorable (not to mention symbolically appropriate, since gold is traditionally assigned to its ruling planet, the Sun). Fortuna Major passes to the tenth house, into a square with the querent's significator, which suggests that the bottles have been moved at some point and will be difficult to find.

A translation, however, forms a link between querent and quesited, since Populus appears in both the twelfth and third houses, forming a conjunction with each of the significators. This combination suggests that the bottles were moved a relatively short distance (third house) to a well-hidden place (twelfth house), and that—possibly by seeking someone else's help, a common way of interpreting translations—the treasure can be found.

The movement of Fortuna Major offers a hint of its own to guide the querent's search. Just as the fourth house corresponds to the earth and what lies beneath it, the tenth house corresponds to the sky. The new hiding place is thus likely to be somewhere high up above the ground. One possibility that comes immediately to mind is that the family farm-house may have a concealed attic space where the bottles of gold dust may have been put for safekeeping. Another is that they may have been concealed atop a hill on the family property.

The Witnesses and Judge, for their part, bode well for the search. The Right Witness is Via, the Left Witness Fortuna Minor, and the Judge Fortuna Major itself. Given a willingness to put out the necessary effort, therefore, the querent may well find himself dusting off those bottles in the near future.

PART II

EARTH MAGIC

CHAPTER FIVE

Geomancy and magic

In the Middle Ages and Renaissance, when geomancy was at its height, it was used by everyone from popes to peasants and had no particular connection to what we might now call occultism. The philosophies and ways of looking at the world common at that time allowed for the sort of subtle flow of information that geomancy, like all systems of divination, seeks to tap; from the medieval perspective, geomancy was simply another way of gathering information about the world. Some theologically minded people doubted that it was appropriate for good Christians to study geomancy, but then the same doubts were raised at the same time about such "occult" studies as physics and logic.

The emergence of modern materialist thinking swept all this away. In place of the easy blending of spiritual and material realms that characterized the older ways of thought, the partisans of the new science proclaimed an absolute barrier between matter and spirit, and insisted that all true knowledge about the world had to be found in one way—their way. The established churches of the West had to be tolerated for political reasons, but anything else that strayed across the border between matter and spirit was labeled "superstition" and targeted for attack.

Geomancy was among these, and in the years following the triumph of the new science it dropped from general use in the Western world. Like many aspects of the older approach to the world, though, it was preserved by groups of magicians who countered their exclusion from mainstream culture by going underground. In these groups, the heritage of Western magic, divination, mysticism, and spiritual philosophy was reworked and recombined in a dizzying variety of ways, resulting in much of modern occult lore.

This process of fusion affected geomancy as much as any other branch of the older lore. In the process, geomancy made a series of deep connections with ritual magic. Several branches of magical practice absorbed the geomantic figures as one of their basic symbolic structures, while magical techniques came to play a part in some approaches to geomantic divination.

None of these are essential to the modern geomancer who simply wishes to learn and use geomantic divination; the material in the first four chapters of this book can stand on its own, just as it did in the Middle Ages. Those readers who are interested in the broader realm of magical practice, though, will find that this further extension of geomantic work well repays study and practice.

The second and third methods of preparing for geomantic divination that we will cover in this chapter (the first was covered in chapter 3) make up one aspect of this deeper level of the lore. There are three others that we'll also be exploring. First, there is the art of making and magically consecrating geomantic instruments, which is detailed in chapter 6. Second is the use of the geomantic figures as subjects for magical meditation and as gateways for the practice of clairvoyance, which will be explored in chapter 7. Third is the use of the figures, and of the geomantic sigils made from them, as tools for practical ritual magic—in particular, for sigil magic and the making and consecrating of magical talismans, the subject of chapter 8. Taken together, these three magical applications provide the foundations of a unified system of magic based on geomancy's vision of elemental patterns moving through the deep consciousness of the Earth.

A simple ceremony for preparation

The first of the two methods of magical preparation for geomancy draws on certain elements of the traditional lore of high magic to help make contact with the anima mundi. In magical teachings, there are seven patterns of consciousness that move through the matrix of awareness that, in its material form, we call the Earth. These are linked to the seven planets of ancient astrology, and are called Planetary Spirits.

Each has a name, a symbol or sigil, and a range of human experiences and activities with which it resonates. Each also has an Intelligence, another personified pattern of consciousness that represents the Planetary Spirit's link to higher levels of existence.

Planetary Spirits

Zazel corresponds to the planet Saturn, and resonates with time, death, agriculture and building, abstract thought and philosophy, as well as all things relating to the past. Its Intelligence is Agiel.

Diagram 5-1. Zazel.

Hismael corresponds to the planet Jupiter, and resonates with good fortune, growth and expansion, formal ceremonies and rites of passage, charity, feasting, and advancement in one's profession or in any organization. Its Intelligence is Yophiel.

Diagram 5-2. Hismael.

Diagram 5-3. Bartzabel.

Bartzabel corresponds to the planet Mars, and resonates with competition, war, destruction, surgery, male sexuality, and matters connected with livestock. Its Intelligence is Graphiel.

Sorath corresponds to the Sun, and resonates with power, leadership, positions of authority, success, balance and reconciliation, and sports and games involving physical effort. Its Intelligence is Nakhiel.

Diagram 5-4. Sorath.

Diagram 5-5. Kedemel.

Kedemel corresponds to the planet Venus, and resonates with art, music and dance, social occasions and enjoyments, pleasures, love, the emotions generally, and female sexuality. Its Intelligence is Hagiel.

Taphthartharath corresponds to the planet Mercury, and resonates with learning, messages, communication, all intellectual pursuits, gambling, medicine and healing, trade, economic matters, trickery, deception and theft. Its Intelligence is Tiriel.

Diagram 5-6. Taphthartharath.

Diagram 5-7. Chashmodai.

Chashmodai corresponds to the Moon, and resonates with journeys, the sea, hunting and fishing, biological cycles, reproduction and childbirth, psychic phenomena, dreams, the unconscious and the unknown. Unlike the other Planetary Spirits, it has two higher patterns of consciousness above it: an Intelligence of Intelligences, Malkah be-Tarshishim ve-ad Ruachoth Shechalim, and a Spirit of Spirits, Shad Barshemoth ha-Shartathan.

The first step in this approach to preparing for divination, then, is to select the one of these seven powers that relates most closely to the question you intend to ask. Once you have done this, draw a circle a few inches across on the sand or earth you will be using for the divination, if you are using this traditional method, or on the paper you will be using to record the divination. Then, inside the circle, draw a pentagram as shown in Diagram 5-8, starting from the top point as shown.

Then draw the sigil of the Planetary Spirit governing the question at the center of the pentagram. The final result, shown here with the Sigil of Sorath for the sake of example, should look like Diagram 5-9.

Now concentrate on the symbol you have drawn and, as in the first method of preparation, center your mind on the question you wish the divination to answer. Once you have achieved a state of balanced focus, begin the divination process.

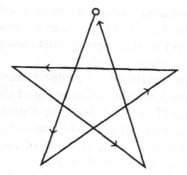

Diagram 5-8. Invoking pentagram.   Diagram 5-9. Planetary Spirit sigil.

After the divination has been completed, the link established between your consciousness and the Planetary Spirit should be released, otherwise that particular aspect of the anima mundi is likely to remain stronger than usual in your life for some time, producing a range of potential imbalances. To close off the link, simply retrace the pentagram in a different way, banishing the forces you have summoned. This is done starting from the bottom left point and going up toward the top point, as shown in Diagram 5-10.

A ritual of high magic

The other method of magical preparation for geomancy we'll be covering here is intended for those who are studying geomancy in the context of a broader course of training in Western high magic, and is most appropriate when used with geomantic instruments that have been magically consecrated according to the method given in chapter 6. Here

Diagram 5-10. Banishing pentagram.

the contact with the anima mundi is mediated through the more intensive processes of Cabalistic magical ritual. As with the other magical
method, the sigil of that one of the seven Planetary Spirits most closely
attuned to the question needs to be chosen beforehand.

This ritual method comprises four distinct rites: the Cabalistic Cross,
the Lesser Banishing Ritual of the Pentagram, the Summoning of the
Planetary Spirit, and the Release of the Planetary Spirit. The Banishing Ritual is performed at the beginning and end of the ceremony, and
the Cabalistic Cross is performed at the beginning and end of each
Banishing Ritual; the total method thus involves eight stages. Not
counting the time spent doing the divination, the whole ceremony takes
about fifteen minutes.

If you are studying a system of magic different from the Cabalistic
system used here, and wish to design a ceremony of your own, this is all
to the good. It's usually best to keep ceremonies of this kind within the
same limits of time and complexity as used here, though, as anything
much longer or more intricate tends to work well only for the most
serious ritual addicts! The Golden Dawn at one point used a divination ritual based on their Neophyte Grade initiation ceremony that took
up to two hours to perform; this is well past the point of diminishing
returns for most magician-diviners.

If you have not learned how to vibrate words of power, this is a preliminary that should not be neglected if you intend to use the method
given here. In magician's jargon, "vibrating" refers to a special way of
intoning or chanting special words in ritual. To learn it, draw in a deep
breath, and then make a steady, drawn-out vowel tone like "aaah." Try
to find a way of doing this that produces a buzzing or tingling sensation
in your chest and throat; play with different ways of shaping the sound
with your mouth and throat, and try to relax into the sound, letting
go of unnecessary tension. With practice, it becomes possible to fill the
entire body with the feeling of vibration, to focus it in a specific part of
the body, and to move it entirely outside the body so that it focuses on
some outside object. For the present purpose, though, this level of skill
isn't necessary; it's enough to be able to get the basic effect when words
need to be vibrated during the ritual.

To perform the ritual, you'll need a private space where you can make
a certain amount of noise without disturbing others. You'll also need a
small cup or goblet of clean water, a stick of incense in a holder, and your
geomantic instruments; if these have been consecrated according to the

method in chapter 6 (or anything similar), they should be wrapped in silk or linen coverings at the beginning of the ritual. The instruments should be in the center of the space, with the cup of water to the north side and the lit incense to the south. Finally, you'll need to take note of the names of the Spirit and its Intelligence, and the sigil of the Spirit.

The ritual itself is performed as follows:

Stage one: the Cabalistic Cross

This stage is intended to center and expand awareness, and open the fundamental channels of energy that are used in magic.

First, stand straight, feet together, arms at sides, facing east, with the geomantic instruments in front of you. Pause, clear your mind, and then visualize yourself expanding upward and outward, through the air and through space, until your body is so large that your feet rest on the Earth as though on a ball a foot across. Raise your right hand above your forehead; draw it down, palm toward your face, visualizing a beam of light descending from far above your head. Touch your fingers to your forehead, and visualize the descending light forming a sphere of pure white radiance, the same size as the Earth beneath your feet, just above the crown of your head. Vibrate the word ATEH (pronounced "ah-teh").

Second, draw your hand down to touch your solar plexus, just below the lower point of the breastbone, and visualize a shaft of light descending from the sphere above your head to the visualized Earth beneath your feet. Vibrate MALKUTH (pronounced "mahl-kooth").

Third, bring your hand back to the center of your chest, and then over to the right shoulder; visualize a beam of light extending from the vertical shaft to a point just past your shoulder, where it forms a sphere of brilliant red light, the same size as the others. Vibrate VE-GEBURAH (pronounced "veh geh-boo-rah").

Fourth, bring your hand straight across from your right shoulder to your left shoulder; visualize a beam of light extending from the vertical shaft to a point just past your left shoulder, where it forms a sphere of brilliant blue light the same size as the others. (At this point, you have visualized a cross of light within your body, with each of its ends forming a sphere.) Vibrate VE-GEDULAH (pro-nounced "veh geh-dyoo-lah").

Fifth, join the hands in front of the center of the chest, fingers together and pointed upward, palms together and flat. Visualize the Earth and the spheres of energy joined by the cross of light. Vibrate LE-OLAM, AMEN (pronounced "leh o-lahm, ah-men").

Stage two: the Lesser Banishing Ritual of the Pentagram

This stage is intended to clear away unwanted patterns of energy from the space so that you can attune yourself to the anima mundi in a state of greater clarity.

Sixth, step to the eastern edge of the space where you're performing the ceremony. With the first two fingers of your right hand extended (the index and the middle fingers), the last two (the pinky and ring fingers) and the thumb folded back into the palm (the sword hand position), and the arm itself held straight, trace a pentagram (as shown in Diagram 5-10) some three feet across in the air before you. This should be made as even and exact as possible. As you trace them, visualize the line drawn by your fingers shining with blue-white light.

When you have finished tracing the pentagram, point to the center of the pentagram and vibrate the Name YHVH (pronounced "yeh-ho-wah").

Seventh, holding your arm extended, trace a line around a quarter circle to the southern edge of the space, visualizing that line in the same blue-white light. Trace the same type of pentagram in the south, with the same visualization; point to the center, and vibrate the Name ADNI (pronounced "ah-dough-nye").

Eighth, trace the line around a quarter circle to the western edge of the space and repeat the process, this time vibrating the Name AHIH (pronounced "eh-heh-yeh"). Then trace the line around a quarter circle to the north and repeat, this time vibrating the Name AGLA (pronounced "ah-geh-lah").

Ninth, trace the line back around to the east, completing the circle. You are now standing inside a ring drawn in visualized light, with a pentagram shining in each of the four quarters. Return to the center and face east, as you were at the opening, but raise your arms to the sides like the arms of a cross, palms forward. Say aloud:

"Before me, Raphael (pronounced "ra-fa-ell"); behind me, Gabriel ("gah-bree-ell"); to my right hand, Michael ("mee-ka-ell"); to my left hand, Auriel ("oh-ree-ell"). For about me flame the pentagrams, and upon me shines the six-rayed star!"

While naming the archangels, visualize them as conventional winged angelic figures, larger than human height and blazing with light. Raphael wears yellow and violet, and carries a sword; Gabriel wears blue and orange, and carries a goblet; Michael wears red and green, and carries a staff; Auriel wears every shade of earth and green growth, and carries a disk bearing a pentagram. When the pentagrams are mentioned, visualize them as clearly as possible. When the six-rayed star is named, visualize a hexagram on the front of your body, about two feet across, the upward-pointing triangle red, the downward-pointing triangle blue, as shown in Diagram 5-11.

Tenth, repeat the Cabalistic Cross, steps one through five above.

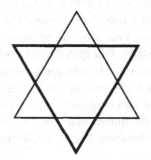

Diagram 5-11. Hexagram.

Stage three: the Summoning of the Planetary Spirit

This stage makes the actual contact with the anima mundi through the symbolic form of the Planetary Spirit you have chosen.

Eleventh, staying inside the circle you have traced in the banishing ritual, unwrap the geomantic instruments and position yourself so that you face north across the surface of the sand or earth. Pick up the cup of water in your right hand, dip the fingers of your left hand into the water, and sprinkle water from your fingers three times onto the earth or sand, saying, "Creature of Earth, I purify thee with water." Set down the cup, pick up the stick of lit incense in your right hand, and wave it three times over the earth or sand, saying, "Creature of Earth, I consecrate thee with fire." Put down the incense, pause, and then pick up the geomantic wand and raise it toward the north, point down. Say: "In and by the mighty Name of God Adonai, I invoke the powers of the living Earth, that I may obtain true knowledge of hidden things."

Twelfth, trace the circle, pentagram, and sigil of the Planetary Spirit on the sand or earth before you, exactly as in the second method of preparation given above; the pentagram should be traced in the direction shown in Diagram 5-8. Then direct the point of the geomantic wand toward the sigil in the center of the pentagram, and say: "And in and by that great Name, and in and by the name of thy Intelligence, (name of Intelligence), I call thee forth, (name of Planetary Spirit), and charge thee to guide my hand truly in this work, that the secrets known to the living Earth may be revealed to me."

Thirteenth, still directing the wand toward the sigil, focus your awareness on the question you seek to answer, as in the two previous methods of preparation. You may have the definite sense, as you do this, that another presence is watching the question take shape, and from a magical point of view this is exactly what is going on—the Planetary Spirit, one aspect of the deep consciousness of the Earth, is becoming aware of the question in your mind. Once the state of focus has been solidly established, begin the divination process.

Stage four: Releasing the Planetary Spirit

This stage releases the link between your awareness and the Planetary Spirit you have summoned, and closes down the magical energies awakened by the ceremony.

Fourteenth, once the first four figures have been created and written down, direct the point of the geomantic wand toward the sigil of the Spirit again, and say, "In the great Name Adonai, and by the name of thy Intelligence (name of Intelligence), I thank thee, (name of Spirit), and bid thee depart. Go in peace, may there be peace between us, and be thou very ready to return when summoned by the mysteries of the Magic of Light." Then trace the pentagram in the banishing direction, as shown in Diagram 5-10, to break the link, and smooth the sand or earth with your hand.

Fifteenth, wrap up your geomantic instruments in their silk or linen wrappings. Then perform the complete Lesser Banishing Ritual of the Pentagram, exactly as given above in steps one through ten, beginning and ending with the Cabalistic Cross. This completes the ceremony.

CHAPTER SIX

Consecrating instruments

According to the Cabalistic philosophy central to many traditions of magic, all the things we experience are simply forms taken by the flowing energies of the inner realms of consciousness. An object that lost all connection to these energies would stop existing at once; everything in the universe of our experience, therefore, is filled with some energy or combination of energies. Different things are connected more or less intensely with these magical energies, however, and link up with their source energies in more or less pure forms. As a result, some things function as effective channels through which power can be tapped and put to use by the magician; other things have much less to offer in this regard.

One of the major approaches to magic, traditionally known as natural magic, relies on those things that are naturally good channels for magical forces—gemstones and crystals, pure metals, many aromatic plants, and so on. This approach is useful for many purposes, but it can have practical drawbacks, especially when the cost or physical properties of these natural channels get in the way. (For example, pure gold is perhaps the best of all channels for the magical energies of the Sun, but not many magicians can afford to spend hundreds of dollars on the raw material for a solar talisman!) A different approach, that of ritual magic, allows this problem to be bypassed. Instead of relying on materials that have a natural link with the energies that are wanted, the ritual magician calls up those energies by way of ceremonial methods and links them with the object.

In the technical language of modern magic, this process of establishing a resonance between a physical object and a magical energy is called *consecration*. To consecrate something magically is to give it an in-dwelling life and energy that will continue to function long after the ritual of consecration is finished—generally as long as the thing in question remains in existence, or until it is deconsecrated by another ceremony. There are a number of standard reasons for consecration workings in modern magic, but one of the most important—and the one central to this chapter—is to make magical working tools of various kinds, charging them with energies that will help the magician to carry out different kinds of work.

Divination is among the classes of magical work that can be assisted in this way, and the various kinds of equipment used for geomantic divination (as discussed in chapter 3) can be consecrated by ritual methods to make them respond to the currents of the anima mundi more easily and precisely. The box and wand are the standard geomantic instruments for consecration and ritual use, and the instructions given here will focus on them; any of the different types, though, can be consecrated using the ceremony given here.

The key to this ceremony, and to all operations of ritual magic, is the combination of focused will, imagination, and effective ritual structure. While rituals usually contain a wide range of words and actions, most of the real work takes place in the consciousness of the magician—which does not mean that the magical forces involved are all in his or her head! Will and imagination are the natural tools by which we handle magical energies, just as hands are the natural tools by which we handle physical objects. The more advanced levels of magical work require the systematic development of will, imagination, and memory, along with all other human capabilities; still, nearly anyone can muster enough of these qualities to perform a basic ritual of consecration effectively.

Making the instruments

The standard set of geomantic equipment for ritual work, as mentioned above, is a box full of sand or earth, and a wand with a sharpened end for making marks in it. While almost any box and stick of convenient size can be used for geomantic divination, the process of consecration puts special conditions on what can be used for consecrated instruments.

The principal requirement is that the materials should be virgin— that is, they should not have been used for any other purpose by human beings. The first use of any object, according to magical lore, shapes the energies present in that object, and this shaping can conflict with the consecration. For this reason, it's usually best to make the box yourself from lumber, unless one of a convenient size can be bought new. The box should be at least ten inches long, eight inches wide, and two inches deep; the upper limit is almost entirely your choice, although a box so wide you can't reach the middle without climbing in is probably too big.

Depending on your skill at carpentry, you may want to make a simple rectangular tray of plywood, or you may choose to make something more elaborate from natural wood; a hinged lid is useful, as it helps to keep the sand or earth where it belongs, and any of the tricks and techniques of the woodworker's craft can be put to use. Whatever your choice and skill level, you should seal all joints with waterproof glue or caulk to keep the contents of the box from leaking out. The surfaces of the box can be left plain or painted—black is traditional for the inside, and the four sides are often painted citrine (a tawny yellow), olive, russet (a rusty red-brown), and black, the symbolic colors of Earth.

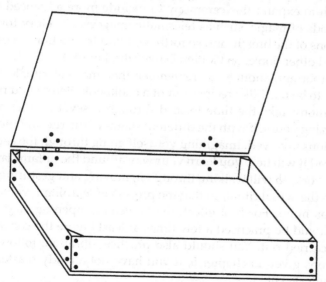

Diagram 6-1. Example of a geomantic box.

The wand can be made from a length of thin doweling, one-fourth to three-eighths inch in diameter and one to two feet long. The point should be sharpened—an ordinary pencil sharpener followed by sandpaper will do the job. If it is painted, it should be white, as it represents the fifth element of Spirit descending into the realm of the four material elements.

The sand or earth that fills the box, finally, should be clean and even-textured, with as little organic material in it as possible. If you use sand that comes from the seashore, wash it thoroughly and allow it to dry in the sun until it is bone dry, in order to keep the energies of the ocean from interfering with what is, after all, a terrestrial method of divination.

Consecrating the instruments

Once you have finished making the box and wand, they should be magically consecrated using a ritual working to link them with the subtle energies of the Earth. There are many different ritual formulae that will accomplish this task, and nearly all systems of magic contain ceremonies that can be adapted for this purpose. The following ceremony, which is derived from consecration rituals used in the Golden Dawn tradition, is one example of an effective way of handling this work; I have adapted and simplified it slightly so that it can be performed with good effect by those who have little or no previous magical experience. (Those who wish to expand this ceremony to include more advanced technical methods of magic, such as telesmatic imagery, vibratory formulae, circulations of the breath, and so forth, will find instructions in *Circles of Power* and other books on Golden Dawn ritual work.)

It's important, though, to remember that magical rituals are not intended to be used like recipes out of a cookbook. Before you perform this ceremony, take the time to read through it several times at least, familiarizing yourself with the different stages of the rite and the words and motions involved. Imagining yourself going through the ceremony as you read it will help you learn your way around the unfamiliar world of ritual work; so will walking through it, moving and gesturing as you would in the actual ritual, so that the process of learning involves body as well as mind. For best effect, the banishing, opening, and closing rituals should be practiced a few times at least before the consecration itself is carried out. You should also practice vibration, following the instructions given in chapter 5, if you have not already mastered this basic magical skill.

When you are ready to perform the ceremony, you will need a private room where you can be undisturbed for up to an hour. Other requirements include a small table or nightstand to serve as an altar, with a black cloth to cover it; a stick of incense—preferably frankincense, which is a good general scent for magical work—in a holder; a cup or goblet of water; and, of course, your geomantic instruments. Candles for lighting and a robe or other magical vestment are also useful additions. The instruments, incense, and cup of water should be on the altar before you begin.

The ceremony of consecration

The first phase of the ceremony is the opening ritual, which brings magical energies into play in the space cleansed by the banishing.

The ritual of opening

First, perform the Lesser Banishing Ritual of the Pentagram, beginning and ending with the Cabalistic Cross, exactly as described in chapter 5.

Second, pause, and then take the cup of water in both hands, raising it up above the level of your head. Say: "And so therefore first that priest who governeth the works of Fire must sprinkle with the lustral waters of the loud-resounding Sea." Lower the cup, and take it to the eastern point of the space. With the cup, draw an equal-armed cross (see Diagram 6-2) in the air to the east; this should be about the same

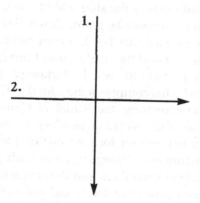

Diagram 6-2. Equal-armed cross.

size, and in the same position, as the pentagram drawn in the banishing, and should be visualized in deep blue. Then dip the fingers of your left hand into the cup and flick water three times to the east.

Third, go around to the south—without tracing a circle around the arc, as in the pentagram ritual—and repeat the process in the south, tracing the cross and sprinkling the water. Do the same to the west, and then to the north. Finally, return to the east, raise the cup high, and say, "I purify with water." Return to the west side of the altar and put the cup back in its place.

Fourth, take the stick of incense from its holder and, holding it in both hands, raise it up above the level of your head. Say: "And when, after all the phantoms are banished, thou shalt see that holy formless Fire which darts and flashes at the hidden depths of the universe, hear thou the voice of Fire." Lower the stick of incense and go to the east; trace an equal-armed cross, like the one you made with the cup, and wave the incense three times to the east. The cross should be visualized as brilliant red. Go around in the same way to south, west, and north, repeating the action, and then return to the east; raise the stick of incense high, and say, "I consecrate with Fire." Return to the altar and put the stick back in its holder.

Fifth, go around the left of the altar to the east, and then slowly circle around the space clockwise three times. As you circle, imagine yourself climbing a spiral stair, while the altar and its implements, the pentagrams and crosses traced around you, and the floor beneath you all rise with you. As you reach the east at the end of the third circuit, imagine yourself reaching the top of the stair.

Sixth, return to the west side of the altar and face east. Raise your arms above the altar and instruments, palms down. Say: "Holy art Thou, Lord of the Universe. Holy art Thou, whom nature has not formed. Holy art Thou, the vast and the mighty one, Lord of the Light and of the Darkness." As you say the word "darkness," lower your hands and bow your head. This completes the Ritual of Opening.

The core of the ceremony, the Ritual of Consecration, follows. During this portion of the working, as much of your will and attention as possible must remain focused on the idea of consecrating the geomantic instruments, charging them with power and opening up connections between them and the subtle forces of the anima mundi. Experienced magicians learn and practice ways to amplify and focus such an act of will, but the intention itself—if focused and held strongly—is enough to energize the ritual forms and success-fully consecrate your geomantic instruments.

The ritual of consecration

Seventh, move around the altar until you are standing south of it, fac-ing north over the geomantic instruments. Take up the cup of water and sprinkle water with your fingers thrice over the instruments, saying, "Instruments of the geomantic art, I purify thee with Water." Then wave the stick of incense three times over the instruments, say-ing, "Instruments of the geomantic art, I consecrate thee with Fire."

Then, with your right hand in the sword hand position described in chapter 5, trace the invoking pentagram of Earth (as shown in Diagram 6-3) in the air above the altar, as though the pentagram were standing on the geomantic instruments. The pentagram should be two to three feet across.

Diagram 6-3. Invoking pentagram of Earth.

Point to the center of the pentagram with your sword hand, and vibrate the Name ADNI (pronounced "ah-dough-nye") ten times. Do this slowly and with maximum concentration, focusing on the sound of the Name as you vibrate it.

Eighth, repeat the following invocation. Names of God written in all capitals (such as ADNI), but none of the other words, should be vibrated.

"O Thou who art from everlasting, Thou who hast created all things, and doth clothe Thyself with the forces of Nature as with a gar-ment, by Thy holy and divine Name ADNI (pronounced "ah-dough-nye"), whereby Thou art known especially in that quarter we name

Tzaphon, the north, I beseech Thee to grant unto me strength and insight for my search after the hidden light and wisdom.

"I entreat Thee to cause Thy wonderful archangel Auriel, who governeth the works of Earth, to guide me in the pathway; and furthermore to direct Thine angel Phorlakh (pronounced "for-lakh") to watch over my footsteps therein. May the ruler of Earth, the powerful prince Kerub, by the gracious permission of the infinite Supreme, increase and strengthen the hidden forces and occult virtues of these instruments so that through them I may be enabled to perform aright those operations for which they have been fashioned. For which purpose I now perform this rite of consecration in the divine presence of ADNI."

Ninth, trace the invoking hexagram of Saturn (as shown in Diagram 6-4) over the altar to invoke the planetary energies, and then repeat the following invocation of the seven planetary spirits. Once again, only the Names of God (in capitals) are to be vibrated. The spirits can be visualized, while you perform this invocation, as shadowy presences gathering outside the circle of pentagrams you traced in the banishing ritual. Say:

"And in and by the seven holy Names of God which govern all the powers of the seven planets, and all their reflections within the body, life, and soul of the Earth, I summon thee, thou seven spirits who art placed over the operations of the art of geomancy, to attend on this ceremony, whereby I do now consecrate these geomantic instruments.

"In the Divine Name YHVH ALHIM (pronounced "yeh-ho-wah ell-oh-heem"), and by the name of thy Intelligence Agiel ("ah-gee-ell"), I summon thee, Zazel ("zah-zell"). In the Divine Name AL

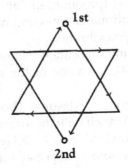

Diagram 6-4. Invoking hexagram of Saturn.

("ell"), and by the name of thy Intelligence Yophiel ("yo-fee-ell"), I summon thee, Hismael ("hiss-mah-ell"). In the Divine Name ALHIM GBVR ("ell-oh-heem ge-boor"), and by the name of thy Intelligence Graphiel ("grah-fee-ell"), I summon thee, Bartzabel ("bar-tzah-bell"). In the Divine Name YHVH ALVH VDAaTh ("yeh-ho-wah ell-oh-wah vah da-ath"), and by the name of thy Intelligence Nakhiel ("nah-khee-ell"), I summon thee, Sorath ("so-rahth"). In the Divine Name YHVH TzBAVTh ("yeh-ho-wah tza-ba-oth"), and by the name of thy Intelligence Hagiel ("hah-gee-ell"), I summon thee, Kedemel ("keh-deh-mell"). In the Divine Name ALHIM TzBAVTh ("ell-oh-heem tza-ba-oth"), and by the name of thy Intelligence Tiriel ("tee-ree-ell"), I summon thee, Taphthartharath ("taf-thar-thar-ath"). In the Divine Name ShDI AL ChI ("shah-dye ell khye"), by the name of thy Intelligence of Intelligences Malkah be-Tarshishim ve-ad Ruachoth Shechalim ("mal-kah veh tar-shish-im veh-ad roo-akh-oth shay-khahl-im"), and by the name of thy Spirit of Spirits Shad Barshemoth ha-Shar-tathan ("shahd bar-shay-moth ha-shar-tah-than"), I summon thee, Chashmodai ("khah-sh-mo-dye").

"Thou seven spirits who art placed over the art of geomancy! Bestow upon these geomantic instruments the subtle powers of Earth, which thou controllest, that this outward and material form may remain a true vessel of inward and spiritual force; and guide my hand in their use, so that thereby I may obtain true knowledge of hidden things through the practice of the geomantic art. Let a secret link be made between these instruments and the hidden forces of Earth, that I may call forth wisdom from the Earth for all just and benevolent purposes."

Tenth, stretch your hands out over the instruments, and say in a slow and distinct voice, "By all the names and powers already invoked, I consecrate and dedicate these instruments to the mysteries of the geomantic art." As you say this, visualize energy rushing in from all directions into the instruments, flooding them with power. This is the climax of the ceremony, and should be done with as much concentration and energy as possible. The visualization, and the act of will it expresses, should be continued at full force for some minutes, or until your focus begins to weaken.

Eleventh, pause, and then say: "In the Name ADNI ("ah-dough-nye"), I proclaim that these geomantic instruments have been truly consecrated!" Then wrap the geomantic instruments in their silk or linen wrappings.

This completes the consecration. At this point the core work of the ceremony is done. The magical energies awakened in the working, though, have to be returned to their ordinary state, and so does the consciousness of the magician performing the rite. The Ritual of Closing, which follows, takes care of both these tasks.

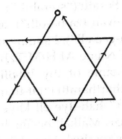

Diagram 6-5. Banishing hexagram of Saturn.

Diagram 6-6. Banishing pentagram of Earth.

The ritual of closing

Twelfth, trace the banishing hexagram of Saturn and then the banishing pentagram of Earth, as shown in Diagrams 6-5 and 6-6, above the altar. Then move around the instruments until you are standing west of them, facing across them to the east, and perform the purification by water and consecration by fire again, exactly as in the second, third, and fourth parts of the ceremony given above.

Thirteenth, go around the right side of the altar to the east, and slowly circle around the space three times counterclockwise. As you are circling, visualize yourself descending the spiral staircase you climbed in the opening, and see the altar and implements, the crosses and pentagrams, and the floor itself descending with you.

Fourteenth, at the end of the third circuit, return to the west side of the altar, face east, and extend your arms to your sides in the form of a cross. Say, "In the great Name of strength through sacrifice, YHShVH YHVShH (pronounced "yeh-hesh-oo-wah   yeh-ho-wah-shah"), I now release any spirit which may have been imprisoned by this ceremony. Depart in peace unto your habitations, and peace be between us, now and in time to come."

Fifteenth, perform the Lesser Banishing Ritual of the Pentagram, as given in chapter 5 and as done at the beginning of the ceremony. This clears away any unwanted energies remaining in the space, and brings the working to a balanced close.

Once you have consecrated a set of geomantic instruments, they should never be touched by any other person and they should normally be kept wrapped in silk or linen, which will insulate them against disruptive energies. The box should also be stored in a place where sunlight will not touch it, because the energies of sunlight will tend to disperse the energies of the consecration. You should use the instruments to perform a divination at least once a week for the first few months after they are consecrated, so that the magical link you have formed with the energies of Earth will be confirmed and solidified, and when doing so you should always use the full ritual method of preparing for divination given in chapter 5.

CHAPTER SEVEN

Meditation and scrying

In the modern West, there's a tendency to think of meditation as something exotic and Eastern, but this is yet another example of the way in which our culture has lost track of its own spiritual and magical roots. The Western world's spiritual traditions contain a very substantial body of lore concerning meditation and closely related practices. This is true of the older mainstream religions such as Catholic Christianity and Judaism, both of which have their own thoroughly developed systems of meditative practice; it's equally true of many of the living traditions of Western magic.

One important difference separates most of these Western approaches to meditation from their Asian equivalents, and from those more recent systems created in the West but based on Eastern models. Although there are exceptions, most of the methods of meditation devised in southern or eastern Asia work by stopping the normal flow of thoughts and impressions through the awareness of the meditator. By fixing the attention on one thing or another—a repeated mantra, a visualization, a cycle of breathing, or bare attention itself—the mind is emptied of thought, so that consciousness can return to its root in the unknown.

Most Western meditative practices, by contrast, seek the same goal in a different way. The thinking process is not stopped but redirected and clarified; thoughts are not abolished but made into a vehicle for the deeper movement of consciousness. This is typically done by turning the mind to a specific topic and allowing it to follow the implications of that topic through a chain of ideas, while at the same time keeping it focused on the topic without straying. By doing this, the Western meditator gradually transforms thinking from half-random mental chatter into a powerful and focused way of understanding; at the same time, the knowledge that comes out of meditation of this sort can have a good deal of value on its own terms.

This last point has made meditation a central practice in many traditions of Western magic, and for good reason. Much of the lore of magic in the West is passed on in the form of complex symbolic patterns, displayed in the initiation rituals of magical lodges or simply studied in books on the subject. These patterns rarely give up their secrets to a casual glance, and because they are patterns of meaning and ways of understanding the world rather than, say, propositions or dogmatic statements about what is true and what is not, trying to turn them into ordinary language and pass them on in a more straightforward way basically doesn't work. The real secrets of magic, it's been said truly, could be shouted from the rooftops without anyone in the world being the wiser.

Of the methods used in Western magic to open up the secrets of these symbolic patterns, meditation is far and away the most important. For example, when a magician meditates on some part of the Tree of Life— the great teaching diagram of Cabalistic magic—he or she recalls the symbols and ideas associated with the Sphere or Path of the Tree in question, tracing out their interactions and allowing them to direct the thinking process along new channels. With time and much practice, this leads to an ability to "think" the Tree, to see the world using the Tree as a lens—and thus to act in ways that rise out of this way of looking at the world, ways that move in harmony with the natural patterns and currents of magical force.

This same approach can be used with any balanced and meaningful structure of symbolism—*and the geomantic figures are such a structure.* Although they have seen little of this kind of use in recent centuries, they were once an important key to understanding the world in a magical way, and they can still be used effectively for this purpose today. Within the sixteen figures of geomancy lies a deep and far-reaching pattern of interaction among the four elements of ancient magical philosophy, one that has a good deal to teach about the spiritual but can also be applied to the details of everyday life with good results.

The same pattern, finally, has much to say concerning the inner side of divination. Each geomantic chart is, in a certain sense, a snapshot of one set of possibilities arising from this pattern, and a sense of the pattern itself—even if this sense is imperfect, as it may be, and word-less, as it must be—provides the deeper context of meaning within which all geomantic readings take shape. On a more pragmatic level, meditation on the geomantic figures is perhaps the best of all ways to learn the figures and their symbolism thoroughly, and thus the best way to see to it that the messages of each chart can be opened up, read, and understood.

Preliminaries to meditation

The first step on the way to meditation is a matter of learning to enter a state of relaxed concentration. The word *relaxed* needs to be kept in mind here. Too often, what concentration suggests to modern people is a kind of inner struggle—teeth clenched, eyes narrowed, the whole body taut with useless tension—that is the absolute opposite of the state you need to reach. The following exercise will help you begin to learn how to reach the more appropriate state as a preliminary to medi-tation on the geomantic figures.

The fourfold breath

For this exercise, you'll need a quiet and not too brightly lit room to work in, and a chair with a straight back and a seat of a height that will permit your feet to rest flat on the floor and keep your thighs level. You'll also need a clock or watch, placed so you can see it easily without moving your head. Sit on the chair with your feet and knees together, your back straight but not stiff, your hands resting on your thighs. Your eyes should be open, looking ahead but not focusing on anything in particular.

Take a few moments to be aware of your physical body. Start at the top of your head and work your way downward to the soles of your feet. Pay special attention to the tensions you feel. Don't try to relax them, or to change them in any way; simply be aware of them. Over time, this simple act of awareness will weaken and eliminate your body's tension patterns by bringing to consciousness the rigidities of thought and emotion that underlie them. Like so much in meditation, however, this process must be allowed to move at its own pace.

Throughout all of this, and all meditative work, keep as still as possible, without fidgeting or shifting, but without forcing stiffness on yourself. Habits of inattention and tension will gradually show up in the form of itches, cramps, and so on, and these obstacles will often become more intrusive as time goes on—for a while. Eventually, if you persist at the practice, the body learns to relax into the position of meditation, and these difficulties come to an end.

When you have finished assessing your physical body, turn your attention to your breathing. Draw in a deep, slow, even breath, while counting mentally from one to four; hold the breath, counting from one to four; let the breath out, slowly, counting from one to four; finally, hold your lungs empty, counting from one to four. Begin again with the in-breath and the count. When holding your breath, don't close your throat; the breath should be held in or out with the muscles of the chest. All breathing should be done through the nose, and the mouth should be gently closed, with the tongue resting against the roof of the mouth.

While you are breathing, your mind will want to run off along various trains of thought. Don't let it. Keep your awareness on the rhythm of the breathing, the feeling of the air moving into and out of your lungs. Whenever your mind slips off into some variety of chatter, as it almost certainly will, bring it gently back to your breathing, and when it slips off again, bring it back again. With practice, you will find yourself able to keep it in place for a moment here and there, and in those moments you will find an odd kind of calm but watchful clarity arising. This is the state you are trying to achieve. Don't be upset if it disappears as soon as you become aware of it. Return to the exercise, and in time the clarity will reappear.

In the first five to ten practice sessions, you should do this exercise for at least five minutes by the clock. Thereafter, ten minutes should be the minimum. Any more than twenty minutes would probably be too much at this point.

Geomantic meditation

Once this preliminary exercise has been practiced often enough that you can reach the state of relaxed concentration with a fair degree of reliability, you are ready to go on to practice meditation itself. Start by turning back to chapter 2, where the sixteen geomantic figures and their symbolism are discussed. Read the entry for the first figure, Puer, and then put the book down. Sit in the posture described above, spend a minute reviewing your body's tensions, and then begin the fourfold breath. During this first part of the practice, you should not think about the figure or, for that matter, anything else. Simply be aware of the rhythm of your breathing, and allow clarity to establish itself.

Maintain this for five minutes or so, and then change from the fourfold breath to ordinary, slow breathing. Picture the figure Puer in your mind's eye, as though it stood hovering in the air in front of you, and begin thinking about its meaning. Recall as many of the correspondences as possible, and try to see how they relate to one another. Go on to think about the idea of the figure in a general way, without allowing your mind to wander off the subject. Finally, out of the various ideas or images that have arisen, choose one train of thought and follow it carefully out to its end. Again, keep your mind on the subject; if it wanders away, bring it gently back and keep going.

Spend between ten and fifteen minutes at this, then return to the fourfold breath for a minute or two. When your mind is again clear, end the practice session. Be sure to write down the images and ideas that came up in the meditation; you are likely to find them useful later on, as you continue your meditations or cast and interpret geomantic charts. It's useful, in fact, to keep a geomantic journal, in which you record your divinations, your meditations, and your other geomantic work for future reference.

In your next meditation session, take the second figure, Amissio, as the focus; visualize it in the air in front of you when you have finished the fourfold breath, and explore its symbolism and meaning. In the following session, work on Albus, and go on in this way through all sixteen figures. You are likely to find that one session per figure barely scratches the surface of what can be learned through meditation on them, but it makes a useful beginning. Once this is completed, go on to work with the figures in greater depth, devoting more time to them as needed, and when this is done meditate on their combinations and relationships with one another—the way two figures add together to make a third, the ways that a given element relates to the different figures it rules, and so on.

How far along this path you go is entirely a matter of how much time and effort you're willing to put into meditative work. Meditating every day, usually at a set time each day, is one of the basic training disciplines for serious students of magic, though not everyone who wants to explore the possibilities of geomantic meditation will fall into this category.

The art of scrying

Another discipline closely related to meditation, and practiced intensively in many Western magical traditions, is the art of scrying. Scrying originally meant seeing in the ordinary sense—the closely related word *descry*, meaning "to sight at a distance," still gets some use in modern English—but scrying was adopted many years ago as a term for a very special kind of seeing that does not rely on the physical eyes.

To understand scrying, it's necessary to know a little about the magical understanding of consciousness. To most people in the Western world nowadays, consciousness is an odd phenomenon that happens entirely inside human brains; each consciousness is cut off from all others, except for whatever indirect link can be managed through material means—speech, writing, skin contact, and so on. This notion comes out of the central dogma of modern thought, the claim that everything that is real is material, that there is nothing in the universe but matter and energy in various states and combinations.

In the magical traditions of the West, things are understood in a completely different way. To the magician, consciousness is what's real, and "matter" is simply our way of talking about the things we perceive through one particular channel—the channel based on our five ordinary senses. There are other channels, including many of the things we usually dismiss as "just in our heads." One of them is the imagination.

Few human capabilities have been as roundly dismissed in our present culture as this one. To call something "imaginary" nowadays is to label it as unreal and unimportant. Magicians know, however, that the imagination is in some ways the most important power human beings have. Imagination is the ability to reshape our experiences into new forms. It's by way of imagination that we assemble the flurry of experiences around us into a world that can be comprehended; it's by way of imagination that we can reshape that world—by using imagination to guide our physical actions, for example, and making something no one has ever made before.

But the core of the magical understanding of imagination is the idea that *the world experienced through imagination is as real as the world experienced through the physical senses.* If you build up an image in your mind's eye—for example, the image of a geomantic figure, or of a pentagram in a banishing ritual—that image is as real, in its own realm, as a rock or a tree in this one. Similarly, if you perceive an image that you have not created—for example, if the image of one of the geomantic figures appears before you in a daydream, or while you are studying the figures and staring off into space—what you are perceiving is a reality. The image and, say, this book don't exist in the same realm, but they do both exist, and both can be a source of information to the perceiving mind.

The realm in which images, dreams, and symbols exist is called the astral plane in many magical writings. The full body of magical lore concerning this realm isn't necessary for our present purpose, and may be studied in books on the philosophy and theory of magic. What should be kept in mind here is that this part of the universe of our experience is a reality in its own right, and one that has much to teach. The astral plane is the natural source and home of symbolism; all symbols are born there, and link up through that realm to the higher or deeper energies that give them their meaning and power. By learning to enter that realm in awareness, magicians draw much of their insight into symbols and their effects.

There are various ways to open up conscious contact with this realm of experience. Most people have heard of astral projection, which is the difficult but useful art of separating the astral part of the individual human being from the lower, more physical aspects. There are also methods of trance that have similar effects, ways of bringing consciousness into the experience of dreams, and approaches in which crystals, dark mirrors, or reflective liquids serve as gateways to the necessary state of consciousness.

The simplest and safest of the various methods, though, involves learning to use the same sort of imaginative ability we all use for daydreams and similar experiences. Just as the kind of meditation discussed above redirects and clarifies thinking, this method—*scrying in the spirit vision*, to give it its full technical name—redirects and clarifies the play of imagination. As with meditation, too, the art of scrying can be usefully turned to the task of opening up the inner worlds of the geomantic figures' meaning.

Geomantic scrying

The basic framework for practicing scrying is the same as the one used for meditation. Begin by taking the meditation posture, review the state of your physical body, and then clear your mind with several minutes of the fourfold breath. Next, visualize the figure you intend to explore as though it was marked on a double door in front of you, and hold this image as clearly as possible in your mind. Then, slowly, visualize the door swinging open until you can see what lies beyond it. Allow the scene beyond, whatever it is, to become clear in your mind's eye.

Now, slowly and clearly imagine yourself rising from your chair, walking up to the doorway, and passing through it. The door remains open behind you, and your physical body remains seated in the chair. Look around at the realm beyond the door, and allow yourself to notice as many details as you can. Then, as soon as you feel ready, imagine yourself walking in whatever direction seems most interesting.

When you decide to bring the scrying to an end, imagine yourself stopping and turning around, then walking back along the way you came. Visualize each of the landmarks you passed on the way in and pass them by, just as if you were retracing your route along a physical path. When you come to the door again, walk through it and feel yourself sitting back down in your chair, returning to your physical body. Watch the door swing slowly but firmly closed. Concentrate on this image for a few moments, then clear your mind with several cycles of the fourfold breath before ending the practice.

You may find yourself a little disoriented afterward; if so, try eating something. Very few things close down the visionary senses more thoroughly than food in the stomach. It can also be useful to move around and to do routine activities, such as washing dishes, to help reorient the awareness back to the material level of experience.

Scrying and meditation

There are important links between scrying and meditation, and they have a direct bearing on the scrying process. Meditation is one of the central practices of magic, scrying is a development from it, and the depth and value of your experiences in scrying will be in large part a function of the extent to which you ground these in meditation.

This has two aspects. On the one hand, the mental training of meditation is the most important single skill that can be brought to the scrying process; the more effectively you can focus your attention and keep interior chatter from interfering with the imagery, the more vivid and powerful your scryings will become. The basis of scrying, as we've seen, is the useful fact that our consciousness is not limited to the inside of our heads, and so a mind focused on a particular pattern of symbolic meaning can tap into wider resources of images and information in harmony with that pattern. The other side of this principle, though, is that an unstable focus can produce unstable results. If your attention wanders, as it likely will, the stray thoughts bring in their own trains of related images, in just the same way as the image or topic you intend.

As a result, your early scryings are likely to be a mixture of useful images and useless ones, like a radio signal where the message is mixed with static. There are ways of sorting the two apart, and one of the more useful of them will be covered a little later in this chapter. On the other hand, the more work you put into meditation, the better your focus will be and the less these sorting methods will be needed.

The other major benefit of meditation is that a solid grasp of the traditional symbols of the figure you are exploring will help you to make sense of the experience and to navigate amid what can often be confusing and uncertain imagery. If that grasp of the symbolism has at the same time been communicated to the deep levels of consciousness through meditation, the symbols can become a shared language, linking conscious and unconscious aspects of the self; images from your meditations that surface in scryings can be read and understood with a high degree of clarity, and used as keys to less easily grasped symbols.

For this reason, as mentioned before, it's a good idea to meditate several times at least on any given figure before scrying that figure. It's generally best, in fact, to combine scrying and meditation into a single sequence of practices in which you carry out meditations on the traditional symbolism of each figure, then do a series of scryings on that figure and meditate afterward on the images and events you experience.

This last use of meditation is one of the most valuable, and most often neglected, parts of the scrying process. After your first scryings, in particular, you'll probably find yourself wanting to do another the next day. The proverb about dreams mentioned in chapter 4 applies equally well to scrying, too; scrying a figure and then not interpreting the results is like receiving a letter and then not opening it. It's best to spend at least two or three meditation sessions going over the images and events of the scrying, relating them to the other symbols of the figure you were scrying and seeing what light they shed on the meanings of the figure. If you need more time to be sure that you understand the symbols, take it. One scrying that has been fully explored through meditation will be more valuable to you than a dozen you barely comprehend. Only when you feel that you've gotten everything you possibly can out of one scrying should you go on to do another.

Helps to scrying

When done by an experienced magician, scrying becomes an intensely vivid waking dream where symbols come to life and are fleshed out by personal knowledge and vision. Although it takes time and practice to reach this level of skill, there are steps that even beginners can take to get the most out of scryings.

The most important of these can be summed up in the old Rosicrucian motto *Festina lente*—"make haste slowly." Take scryings, and all practices of this sort, at your own speed, and never go further in any scrying than you're comfortable going. In your first few scryings, you may find it best to go only a short distance beyond the door, and in all cases pay close attention to every image you encounter, no matter how unimportant it seems. If an image appears vague or blurred, pause before it and try to see it with as much clarity as possible. It's important, too, to treat whatever you meet on the figure as real for the duration of the scrying. If you come across the image of a living being, pay attention to what it says; if you encounter a physical object, deal with it as you would a similar object in the material world. The more you behave as though the experiences of the figure are real, the more real they will become for you.

One caution must be made about your dealings with the apparently living beings you may encounter during a scrying. Some of these are honest and will teach you things of value, but others are not and will try to deceive you. Some people find it difficult to think of "imaginary" beings in these terms, but these entities can be as independent of the scryer's conscious will as the people who appear in dreams; they have a life of their own and can behave in highly unexpected ways. Treat them with the same combination of courtesy and caution you would use toward potentially dangerous strangers.

Testing your experiences

As mentioned above, a certain amount of confusion can creep into scrying due to difficulties with mental focus (and a number of other factors). In order to deal with this difficulty, magicians have invented a number of ways of testing information received in scrying for accuracy. Most of these rely on a detailed mastery of Cabalistic lore too complex to cover here, but there is one method that can be used without this kind of background. This depends on the colors associated with the geomantic figures, as given in chapter 2.

The way to use this method is conveniently simple. While actually doing a scrying, and while considering the results afterward, keep in mind the colors of the figure you are scrying. Objects and entities that appear in these colors are likely to belong in the working, while those with different colors more than likely do not. Thus, for example, if the image of a warrior in red armor appears in a scrying of Puer or Cauda Draconis, he probably belongs there; if the same warrior shows up in a scrying of Populus, his color gives him away as an intruder.

Practicing this method of testing by colors will help to keep your scrying experiences balanced and constructive. Common sense and a sense of humor, though, will do more. Scrying can be a powerful tool for deepening your understanding of the geomantic figures and for opening up some of the hidden possibilities of human awareness, but it can also be an opportunity for many different kinds of foolishness, some of them relatively amusing, some a good deal less so. People have made spectacular blunders by blindly trusting information received from scrying and similar practices in a simple-mindedly literal way, and in extreme cases—which are rare, but not rare enough—the results have included madness and death.

The best way to avoid the pitfalls is to remember that scryings take place in a world of their own, and the information you receive in them may or may not have anything to do with the world of ordinary waking experience. It's also worth remembering that the entities you encounter may resort to lies, flattery, or trickery if that is part of their nature; it's as foolish to trust them unquestioningly as it would be to do the same thing to the first stranger you encounter on the street. Whatever you encounter in scrying should be taken with at least a grain of salt, and put through the filter of thorough and thoughtful meditation after the scrying is over.

CHAPTER EIGHT

Sigils and talismans

The methods of magical practice covered in the last two chapters include some of the more important basic elements of the Golden Dawn magical tradition. At the same time, though, they may have little to do with magic in the sense this word is usually given in the modern world. The generic magicians of fantasy novels, Hollywood movies, and role-playing games rarely spend their time opening up links between divinatory equipment and the anima mundi, say, or brooding over the hidden meaning of symbolic patterns in meditation; their chief interest, and their major plot function, is to cause changes in the world around them through magic.

These magician-figures are caricatures, to be sure, but there is a core of truth behind the glossy exterior. Central to the traditions of Western magic are ways of shaping the world through ritual practice. Granted, no part of these traditions have been so roundly dismissed by the material-minded as the idea that magical actions can have effects on the universe of our daily experience. Still, the scorn of those who have never studied magic, much less attempted to practice it, is hardly relevant here. Not every ritual succeeds—magic is no more omnipotent than any other human way of shaping the world—but successful magical workings are everyday occurrences for practicing magicians.

151

Those who take the time to learn the basics of magical theory and practice, and to put these to work in an intelligent and disciplined way, will quickly learn the truth of the matter for themselves.

There are differences between what magicians can do in movies and the like, of course, and what they can do in the world of our everyday experience. Like divination, magic is a natural process founded on natural laws, and its limits are those of nature. Under natural conditions, for example, people don't usually shoot lightning bolts from their fingertips, and magical training and practice—even years of it—isn't likely to change this fact. It's a very common experience of magicians that the results of their rituals usually come about in apparently ordinary ways, with a minimum of fuss. In fact, magic has sometimes been called the art of causing coincidences to happen in accordance with will—a definition that should give some sense of its extraordinary power, for good or ill.

The basics of magic

The art of ritual magic in the Western magical tradition draws on a very substantial body of teaching—spiritual, philosophical, ceremonial, technical, and practical—which cannot be covered here for sheer reasons of space. Fortunately, a basic set of guidelines can be presented and learned quickly, and these are enough to enable several different types of magical work to be done effectively and safely.

The first principle of magic has already been introduced in this book—the idea that *the most important tools of magic are the human will and imagination.* Most of the intricacies of magical practice, the "woven paces and waving hands," the robes and colors and billowing incense, are there to help focus and direct the will and imagination of the magician toward a single purpose and to place the resulting current of will and imagination in harmony with the broader currents of consciousness that flow through the universe.

The second principle will also come as no surprise to anyone who has been paying attention to the material we've already covered. This is the idea that *will and imagination are most effectively directed through a symbolic structure.* By choosing a particular symbol that is part of a specific set of symbolism, the magician can focus his or her energies with maximum clarity and send them through channels already established in the subtle levels of being.

The third principle has not been discussed yet, but it follows from the two already given. This is the idea that *every magical working needs to have a clearly defined purpose set out in advance.* In order to direct will and imagination, as well as in order to select the symbolism through which these are to be directed, the magician needs to know exactly what changes he or she is trying to bring about in the universe. It's generally best to mull over the purpose of a potential working until you can phrase the whole thing in a single clear sentence that allows for no double meanings or ambiguities.

The fourth principle, finally, derives not from the three we've already covered but from the way these three impact the world of our experience. This is the idea that *every magical action has consequences that affect the magician.* In reality, of course, the word *magical* could be left out of this sentence without making it any less true. People in the modern West have so often tended to use magic as a dumping ground for wish-fulfillment fantasies, though, that the reminder may not be out of place.

There are any number of people, for example, whose first thought concerning the use of magical powers involves getting money without working for it. The problem here is that for one person to get money without working for it, there has to be someone else who works for it without getting it. To seek a free ride for oneself, in other words, is to seek to increase the total amount of economic injustice in the world. Every magical action brings its energies to bear on the magician as well as the target of the working, and so, as the saying goes, what goes around, comes around.

The Sanskrit term *karma,* which denotes a very similar concept in Hindu tradition, is familiar to most people nowadays, and it's worth keeping the word and the idea in mind when considering any magical action. The same principle can be traced equally well in most of the other common corruptions of magic. Using magic to kill or hurt another person, for example, or to control someone else's will—most love spells actually seek this, of course—is a very effective way to bring similar patterns of force to bear on one's own life. Equally, the same effect in reverse governs the more positive applications of magic.

Whatever you try to bring about by magic, be it blessing or curse, affects you as well as your target; before performing any act of practical magic, therefore, it's critical to be sure that you are willing to take the consequences that will follow. Because of considerations like these, most competent magicians tend to keep to a relatively high ethical standard, at least in their magical work, out of sheer self-protection; those who don't, don't generally last long.

The geomantic sigils

The second of the four principles discussed above provides the link between ritual magic and the geomantic lore covered earlier. Any coherent set of symbols can be used as a framework for ritual workings, and the geomantic figures are rich in the kind of correspondences and implications that make for effective ritual use. For this reason, they were borrowed for magical work in the Western tradition by the time of the Renaissance—but borrowed with certain alterations.

There are several basic requirements that symbols must meet to be useful in magical work, and the geomantic figures meet all but one of them. First, magical symbols need to have clear meanings, so that using one will bring a specific, focused energy into play. Second, they need to have a well-developed set of correspondences, so that they can be linked with other symbolic systems in ritual work. Third, they need to have a relatively balanced and comprehensive array of meanings, so that a magician can find at least one that relates to any conceivable magical purpose. Finally, they need to be visually clear and distinct, even in less-than-perfect lighting conditions, so that they can be instantly recognized by sight in the candle-lit dimness of a ritual space.

The geomantic figures meet the first three requirements without difficulty, but for many people they fail the fourth. In their usual form, as collections of dots, they don't communicate visually as well as most other magical symbols. Because of this, magicians have devised sets of stylized images of the figures for use in ritual work. The word "sigil" (from Latin *sigillum*, "seal") is the standard magical term for images of this sort, and so these new forms of the figures are termed the geomantic sigils.

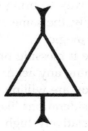

Diagram 8-1. Sigils of Puer.

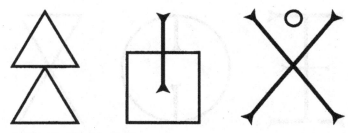

Diagram 8-2. Sigils of Amissio.

Diagram 8-3. Sigils of Albus.

Diagram 8-4. Sigils of Populus.

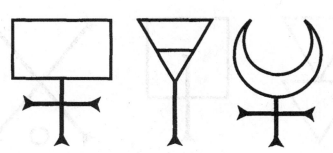

Diagram 8-5. Sigils of Fortuna Major.

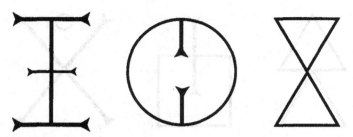

Diagram 8-6. Sigils of Conjunctio.

Diagram 8-7. Sigils of Puella.

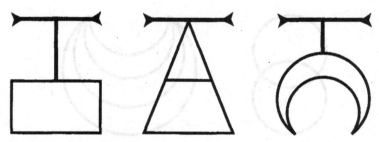

Diagram 8-8. Sigils of Rubeus.

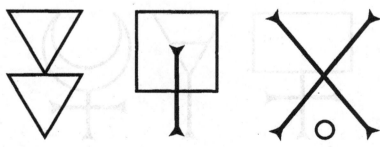

Diagram 8-9. Sigils of Acquisitio.

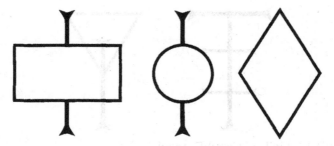

Diagram 8-10. Sigils of Carcer.

Diagram 8-11. Sigils of Tristitia.

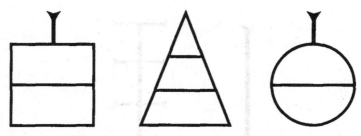

Diagram 8-12. Sigils of Laetitia.

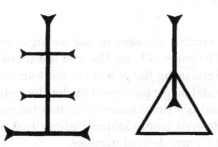

Diagram 8-13. Sigils of Cauda Draconis.

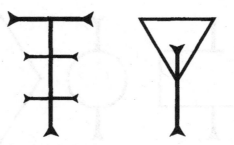

Diagram 8-14. Sigils of Caput Draconis.

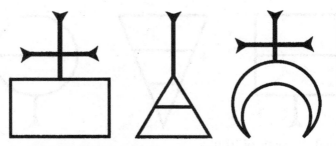

Diagram 8-15. Sigils of Fortuna Minor.

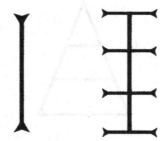

Diagram 8-16. Sigils of Via.

There are any number of ways to use the sigils in practical magic. Two of them will be covered here. The first is a set of rituals for working magic with sigils using the powers of the four elements, based on methods of elemental magic pioneered by the Hermetic magician Franz Bardon. The second is a ritual for consecrating talismans based on the sigils, which is derived from Golden Dawn ritual methods. Each of them can be used for any desired purpose.

Geomantic sigil magic

There is a different sigil ritual for each element, but all four have a basic framework—in magical jargon, a *formula*—in common. This formula can be broken down into four parts:

1: Choosing the sigil

The magician must settle on a specific, clearly stated purpose for the working, select the one out of the sixteen geomantic figures that fits the purpose most closely, and then choose one of the sigils assigned to the figure. There are several ways to help make sure the right energy is being put into the situation; casting a geomantic chart is one good approach, with "What will be the results if I use this sigil?" as the question, and the situation that is to be changed determining the house of the quesited. It's also possible, for those with a solid grasp of the figures and their interrelationships, to work out which figure best symbolizes the situation that needs changing, and then to determine what figure needs to be added to it in order to make a desired outcome, such as Laetitia or Fortuna Major.

2: Preparing the basis

The method described here uses a material basis for the sigil, made of a substance that will interact well with the substance of the element. In order to carry the force of the ritual, the basis will have to be prepared to receive the sigil and the associated energies. This involves preparing a fluid condenser, following the instructions given below.

Making a Fluid Condenser. For all four rituals, you'll need to know how to make a fluid condenser—a substance that effectively absorbs and holds onto magical energies. There are a number of ways to do this, but the easiest (and one of the most effective) borrows a trick from the alchemists and relies on the magical properties of metallic gold.

For the first step, you'll need a small glass or enamel-coated saucepan with a tight lid, one half cup or so of distilled or spring water, and a piece of gold or gold-plated jewelry; since some kinds of jewelry can be damaged by the process that follows, be sure the piece you choose is one you can damage without upsetting anyone. Put the gold and the water in the pan, cover, bring to a full boil, and then let the pan cool to room temperature while still covered. Repeat the process at least half a dozen times, and then remove the gold and set the water aside in a covered jar.

Into the same pan, put two cups of pure water and either a few teaspoons of chamomile flowers, which are readily available from most stores that sell herbs or herbal teas, or the same amount of good-quality black tea leaves. (White lily petals, poplar leaves, white betony or mandrake roots, acacia blossoms or the leaves and flowers of *Arnica montana* can also be used for this purpose, but chamomile or tea work as well and are usually much easier to get.)

Cover the saucepan again and bring to a boil, and keep it boiling for about ten minutes. Take it off the heat and let it cool, then strain the mixture to get the leaves out. Return the liquid to the pan and simmer, uncovered, until half the water has evaporated, then cool to room temperature.

Combine the gold water and the herb water, then, and pour the resulting liquid into a clean glass jar. Seal it tightly and store it in a dark place until you are ready to use it. If the fluid condenser needs to be kept for more than a day or so, measure it and add an equal amount of strong vodka or pure grain alcohol to the mixture to prevent mold.

3: Impressing the sigil

This is the step of the actual ceremony where the sigil is put to work as a frame for magical energies. The tools of will and imagination, the foundations of all magical work, play the central role here. In the context of the rite, the sigil is visualized as intensely as possible, and this visualization is projected onto the material basis.

4: Releasing the sigil

The final step consists of letting go of the energy pattern that has been created, allowing it to get to work. This step involves releasing the image and then, as far as possible, putting the whole subject out of one's thoughts. At the same time, the material basis should be released into the governing element in an appropriate way.

These elemental rituals make a particularly good fit with the geo-mantic sigils, given the deep interconnections between geomancy and elemental lore. Which one you will use in any given case depends on which of the geomantic figures relates most closely to the purpose of your working. The outer element of the figure you select is the element that governs the ritual as well.

Sigil ritual of fire

To make use of the sigils of Puer, Fortuna Major, Acquisitio, and Cauda Draconis, you'll need a piece of watercolor paper, which can be bought at any art store, or any other fairly heavy absorbent paper. You'll also need some of the fluid condenser, an eyedropper, and a source of fire: a candle flame will do, but if a small fire can be made in a safe and secure place outdoors, this is better. Finally, as in any magical working, you'll need to have settled on a purpose for the working in advance, and distilled it down to a single clear sentence.

The ritual itself is performed as follows:

First, light the fire and tend it until it is burning steadily. Say, "In the great Name ALHIM (pronounced "ell-o-heem"), I call forth the powers of Fire."

Second, take the absorbent paper and allow four drops of the fluid condenser to fall on it. As you do this, begin visualizing the sigil you have chosen as though this was drawn on the paper in lines of blazing red light. Hold that image as intensely as you can, for several minutes at least, meanwhile holding the paper close enough to the fire that the fluid condenser begins to dry out.

Third, repeat the purpose of the working once aloud, using the precise words you selected earlier, and at the same moment cast the paper in the fire and watch as it burns, concentrating on the idea that the fiery energies of the sigil are joining with the physical fire, and are able to act wherever fire in any of its forms—flame, heat, light, or any kind of energy—is present in the world.

Fourth, after the paper has burned completely, say, "In the Name ALHIM, I proclaim that this working is complete and that its pur-pose shall be accomplished." Wait until the fire dies down or, if you are using a candle, blow it out. This completes the ritual.

Sigil ritual of air

To make use of the sigils of Albus, Puella, Tristitia, and Fortuna Minor, you'll need a small metal or fireproof ceramic dish, a small amount of the fluid condenser, an eyedropper, and a non-electric heat source: an alcohol lamp of the sort used in chemistry experiments is probably best, but the sort of canned heat used for fondues, a wood stove, or a large candle will do. Some arrangement for holding the dish steady over the flame is also necessary. You'll also need your sentence defining the purpose of the working.

The ritual is performed as follows:

First, light the heat source, and put a little water into the dish, just enough to cover the bottom; leave the dish off the heat for the time being. Say: "In the Great Name YHVH (pronounced "yeh-ho-wah"), I call forth the powers of Air."

Second, add four drops of the fluid condenser to the water. As you do this, visualize the sigil you have chosen as though it was drawn in the water in lines of blazing yellow light. Hold this visualization for several minutes at least.

Third, repeat the purpose of the working once out loud, using the precise words you selected earlier, and at the same moment put the dish over the flame. As the water evaporates, concentrate on the idea that the airy energies of the sigil are uniting with the air all around you, and are able to act wherever air or any gas is present in the world.

Fourth, when the water has all evaporated, say: "In the Name YHVH, I proclaim that this working is complete and that its purpose shall be accomplished." Remove the dish from the heat and extinguish the heat source. This completes the ritual.

Sigil ritual of water

To make use of the sigils of Populus, Rubeus, Laetitia, and Via, you'll need a small container for water, a small quantity of the fluid condenser, an eyedropper, and access to a river, stream, lake, or seashore where you can work the ritual without being observed. Again, you'll need to have settled on the purpose for the working and composed a sentence that expresses it exactly.

The ritual is performed as follows:

First, fill your container with water from the river, stream, lake, or sea before you, and say: "In the Great Name AL (pronounced "Ell"), I call forth the powers of Water."

Second, let four drops of the fluid condenser fall into the water in your container. As you do this, visualize the sigil you have chosen as though it is drawn on the water in lines of blazing blue light. Hold this visualization as intensely as possible for several minutes at least.

Third, repeat the purpose of the working once out loud, using the precise words you selected earlier, and at the same moment pour the water in your container out into the water of the river, stream, lake, or sea. As the waters mingle, concentrate on the idea that the watery energies of the sigil are uniting with the water before you, and are able to act wherever water or any liquid is present in the world.

Fourth, say: "In the Name AL, I proclaim that this working is complete and that its purpose shall be accomplished." This completes the ritual.

Sigil ritual of earth

To make use of the sigils of Amissio, Conjunctio, Carcer, or Caput Draconis, you'll need a small piece of paper, a small amount of the fluid condenser, an eyedropper, a shovel or trowel, and access to a piece of ground where you can bury something safely without being observed. Once more, you'll also need the sentence that expresses the purpose of the working.

The ritual is performed as follows:

First, dig a hole one foot or more deep into the ground. Say: "In the Great Name ADNI (pronounced "ah-dough-nye"), I call forth the powers of Earth."

Second, let four drops of the fluid condenser fall onto the paper. As you do this, visualize the sigil you have chosen as though it was drawn on the paper in lines of blazing green light. Hold this visualization for several minutes at least.

Third, repeat the purpose of the working once out loud, using the precise words you selected earlier, and at the same moment drop the paper into the hole. Fill in the hole and, as you do so, concentrate on the idea that the earthy energies of the sigil are uniting with the earth beneath you, and are able to act wherever earth or any solid thing is present in the world.

Fourth, when the hole is all filled in, say: "In the Name ADNI, I proclaim that this working is complete and that its purpose shall be accomplished." Cover over all traces of the hole so that the soil looks as undisturbed as possible. This completes the ritual.

Talismanic magic

Another kind of magic well suited to the symbolism of geomancy is the construction and consecration of talismans. Talismans are one of several different kinds of devices made and used in Western magical practice, and these are too often confused with one another; for the sake of clarity—an important virtue in magical work—it's worth taking a moment to distinguish among them.

An *amulet*, for example, is a device made from herbs, stones, and other materials according to the rules of natural magic. It is not usually consecrated—instead, its power comes from the natural flow of power through the materials that make it up. A *working tool* (the term *magical weapon* is often used for these) is a consecrated device meant to direct some specific magical energy for use in ritual work. Both of these have a fairly general application in magic; they can be used in a wide range of situations, whenever the specific energies placed in the device are of use.

A *talisman*, by contrast, is a much more specialized device. The energies that have been bound into a talisman are there to accomplish a single purpose, which has been defined by the magician and established by a ritual of consecration. Once consecrated, the talisman keeps projecting its energies toward the fulfillment of its purpose, day in and day out, until it accomplishes its purpose or is ritually deconsecrated by the one who made it. Talismans are thus among the most useful ways of working magic when the task at hand requires persistence or continuous effect.

There are certain corresponding drawbacks to talismans that need to be kept in mind. The most important is that a talisman draws its energy from the life force of the magician who consecrates it. A certain portion

of the magician's vitality must pass into any talisman he or she consecrates and, until the talisman is deconsecrated, this portion of energy
remains linked with the talisman and its purpose. This is rarely a problem when a magician makes one or two talismans, but beginners sometimes run wild with the technique and make dozens—at which point
health problems can start cropping up.

Another potential source of problems comes from the very persistence of effect that makes talismans so valuable as a magical tool. Until
and unless a talisman is deconsecrated, it keeps on working, even if its
effects are no longer needed or even wanted. For this reason, it's generally a bad idea to make talismans and give them to other people, or to
keep them in places where they may get lost. It's possible for an experienced magician to deconsecrate a talisman from a distance, but this is
not work for novices.

Making a geomantic talisman

The process of talismanic magic includes two principal steps; the
talisman has to be made, first of all, and then it has to be consecrated.
The consecration is a ritual process, carried out along much the same
lines as the consecration of the geomantic instruments in chapter 6.
The making of the talisman itself, though, is a somewhat different
matter.

The basic requirements for a talisman are simple, but they do
place certain limitations on the process. On the one hand, talismans
need to be made of a substance that will absorb magical energies and
hold them indefinitely; on the other, they need to be made of a substance that will serve readily as a medium for appropriate symbols,
which are drawn, painted, or carved on the surface. There are only
a few natural materials that meet both these requirements, and the
two commonly used in older traditions of magic—genuine sheepskin
parchment and pure metals—are prohibitively hard for most modern
people to obtain.

Fortunately, there are other options. One of the best is to use a strong
absorbent paper such as heavy watercolor paper, which is available at
most art-supply stores, and paint it with two or three coats of water
in which a piece of gold has been boiled, following the first half of the
recipe for a fluid condenser given above. The paper should be cut into

the desired shape for the talisman before painting, allowed to dry in direct sunlight afterward, and then wrapped in silk or linen to keep it from picking up stray energies.

The next step is the design of the talisman's symbolism. Talismans in Western magical tradition have quite often tended to be cluttered with all manner of symbols, and the geomantic sigils first seem to have entered magical use as one more element to add to the clutter. A simpler approach can also be used, however, and this is the method we'll discuss here.

The design for a geomantic talisman, according to this simpler approach, includes two factors: the color assigned to the geomantic figure and the sigil itself. The color you use should be either the traditional color of the figure or the King Scale color, taken from the tables in chapter 2. Artist's colored pencils, which are readily available, are perhaps the best of the available media for drawing the design. The paper on which the talisman is drawn may be round (the most common shape for talismans in the Western tradition) or square (to refer symbolically to the four elements); the sigil should be drawn in the center, and a colored border around the edge of the talisman, as shown in Diagram 8-17.

Diagram 8-17. Talisman of Fortuna Major.

Once the talisman has been made, it should be consecrated as soon as circumstances allow.

Consecrating a geomantic talisman

The ceremony given here, like the consecration ceremony for geomantic instruments covered in chapter 6, is a simple method based on Golden Dawn magical techniques that can be used effectively by the beginning magician. There are other approaches to the process of consecration, some of them substantially more powerful; readers who are interested in exploring these more intensive methods can find them in a range of texts on ritual magic, including my book *Circles of Power*.

Like the ceremony in chapter 6, this one requires a private space where you can work undisturbed for up to an hour, a small table or nightstand to serve as an altar, a cup of water, and a stick of incense in a holder. A completed talisman, ready to consecrate, is also a necessity! It should be wrapped in silk or linen wrappings, and not taken out until the proper point in the ritual.

A black cloth to cover the altar, and a white robe or the like for the magician, are useful but not necessary. Note the outer element of the geomantic figure that governs the talisman; this will make a difference at certain points in the consecration.

The ceremony consists of an Opening, a Consecration, and a Closing, and is performed as follows:

The ritual of opening

First, perform the Lesser Banishing Ritual of the Pentagram, beginning and ending with the Cabalistic Cross, exactly as described in chapter 5.

Second, pause, and then take the cup of water in both hands, raising it up above the level of your head. Say: "And so therefore first that priest who governeth the works of Fire must sprinkle with the lustral waters of the loud-resounding Sea." Lower the cup, and take it to the eastern point of the space. With the cup, draw an equal-armed cross in the air to the east (see page 147); this should be about the same size, and in the same position, as the pentagram drawn in the banishing ritual, and should be visualized in deep blue. Then dip the fingers of your left hand into the cup and flick water three times to the east.

Third, go around to the south—without tracing a circle around the arc, as in the pentagram ritual—and repeat the process in the south, tracing the cross and sprinkling the water. Do the same to the west, and then to the north. Finally, return to the east, raise the cup high, and say, "I purify with Water." Return to the west side of the altar and put the cup back in its place.

Fourth, take the stick of incense from its holder and, holding it in both hands, raise it up above the level of your head. Say: "And when, after all the phantoms are banished, thou shalt see that holy form-less Fire which darts and flashes at the hidden depths of the universe, hear thou the voice of Fire." Lower the stick of incense and go to the east; trace an equal-armed cross, like the one you made with the cup, and wave the incense three times to the east. The cross should be visualized as brilliant red. Go around in the same way to south, west, and north, repeating the action, and then return to the east; raise the stick of incense high, and say, "I consecrate with Fire." Return to the altar and put the stick back in its holder.

Fifth, go around the left of the altar to the east, and then circle around the space clockwise three times slowly. As you circle, imagine yourself climbing a spiral stair, while the altar, the pentagrams and crosses traced around you, and the floor beneath you all rise with you. As you reach the east at the end of the third circuit, imagine yourself reaching the top of the stair.

Sixth, return to the west side of the altar, and face east. Raise your arms above the altar and talisman, palms down. Say: "Holy art Thou, Lord of the Universe. Holy art Thou, whom nature has not formed. Holy art Thou, the vast and the mighty one, Lord of the Light and of the Darkness." As you say the word "darkness," lower your hands and bow your head. This completes the Ritual of Opening.

The ritual of consecration

Seventh, unwrap the talisman and set it at the center of the altar, keeping a fold of the wrapping between the talisman and your fingers; be careful not to touch any part of it with your bare skin. Take the cup of water, dip the fingers of your left hand in it, and sprinkle a few drops of water three times onto the talisman. Say: "Creature of talismans, I purify you with water." Put down the cup, pick up the incense, and wave it three times over the talisman; say: "Creature of talismans, I consecrate you with fire."

Eighth, move clockwise around the altar, if necessary, until you face the direction of the outer element of the geomantic figure governing the talisman: east for a figure of Air, south for one of Fire, west for one of Water, or north for one of Earth. With the fingers of your right hand in the sword hand position, trace in the air an invoking pentagram of the same element, as shown in Diagram 8-18. Draw the pentagram as though it stood upright on the altar above the talisman, and visualize the lines drawn by your fingers as though you drew them in brilliant white light. Then, in the center of the pentagram, draw the geomantic sigil on the talisman; visualize this in the same color you used for the talisman.

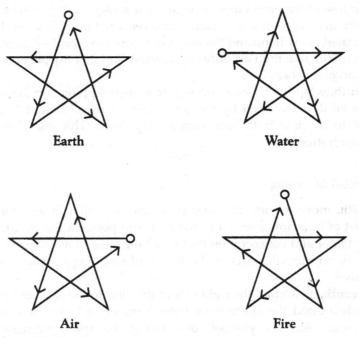

Earth   **Water**

Air   **Fire**

Diagram 8-18. Invoking pentagrams.

Ninth, point to the center of the sigil in the pentagram, and vibrate four times the Name of God governing the element: for a figure of Air, YHVH (pronounced "yeh-ho-wah"); for one of Fire, ALHIM (pronounced "ell-o-heem"); for one of Water, AL (pronounced "ell"); for one of Earth, ADNI (pronounced "ah-dough-nye"). As you do this, concentrate as intensely as possible on the image of the pentagram and the sigil, in their respective colors. Then, holding the image at maximum intensity, lower your hand until you are pointing at the talisman directly, and visualize the pentagram and sigil moving downward until the visualized sigil and the sigil on the talisman fuse and are one.

Tenth, pick up the talisman, keeping a fold of the wrapper between it and your hand, and raise it high up over your head. Bring it down to face level, and breathe on it three times, slowly, concentrating on the idea that energy is passing with your breath into the talisman. Put the talisman down, and say, "Creature of talismans, by the Mighty Name already invoked, I give thee life and power, as flame is lit from flame, for the fulfillment of this purpose ..." At this point repeat the purpose of the working in a single clear sentence. "Let this be done without evasion or equivocation, and cease not until thou art deconsecrated at my hand and thy energies return whence they came. And I proclaim that thou art duly consecrated, and that my purpose shall be accomplished."

Eleventh, wrap the talisman up tightly in its wrappings, so that it will not be deconsecrated by the banishings in the closing; be careful not to touch it with bare skin at any point. This completes the consecration.

The ritual of closing

Twelfth, move around the altar if necessary until you are standing west of it, facing across it to the east, and perform the purification by Water and consecration by Fire again, exactly as in the second, third, and fourth parts of the Ritual of Opening ceremony given above.

Thirteenth, go around the right side of the altar to the east, and slowly circle around the space three times counterclockwise. As you are circling, visualize yourself descending the spiral staircase you climbed in the opening, and see the altar and implements, the crosses and pentagrams, and the floor itself descending with you.

Fourteenth, at the end of the third circuit, return to the west side of the altar, face east, and extend your arms to your sides in the form of a cross. Say, "In the great Name of strength through sacrifice, YHShVH YHVShH (pronounced "yeh-hesh-oo-wah yeh-ho-wah-shah"), I now release any spirit which may have been imprisoned by this ceremony. Depart in peace unto your habitations, and peace be between us, now and in time to come."

Fifteenth, perform the Lesser Banishing Ritual of the Pentagram, as given in chapter 5 and as done at the beginning of the ceremony. This clears away any unwanted energies remaining in the space, and brings the working to a balanced close.

Once the talisman has been consecrated, it should be placed in a covering that will not block the flow of its energies (small manila envelopes seem to work well) and put in a safe place where it will not be disturbed, and where no magical rituals will be performed close by. Once this is done, leave it alone and let the energies of the talisman get to work.

Deconsecrating a geomantic talisman

Once a talisman's work is done, as mentioned above, it needs to be ritually deconsecrated. This is a relatively simple process; the vortex of energies that gives a talisman its life and effect can be disrupted and dispersed by any basic banishing formula. The following short ceremony will accomplish this cleanly and effectively. You will need an altar or some other surface on which to put the talisman, but this is the only requirement.

The ceremony is performed as follows:

First, take the talisman out of its covering, without touching it, and set it at the center of the altar. With your right hand in the sword hand position, point to the center of the talisman, and say: "Creature of talismans, thy work is accomplished. I deconsecrate thee and return thy energies whence they came."

Second, trace the banishing pentagram of the same element you invoked to charge the talisman, as shown in Diagram 8-19. The pentagram should be drawn as though it stood on the altar above the talisman.

Third, perform the complete Banishing Ritual of the Pentagram as given in chapter 5, beginning and ending with the Cabalistic Cross. This completes the ceremony.

Once the talisman has been deconsecrated, it should be disposed of in some way that harmonizes with its ruling element: a talisman of Fire may be burnt, one of Water cast into a river or the sea, one of Air torn to small pieces and scattered from a high place, and one of Earth buried. This allows any remaining elemental energies to return to their sources.

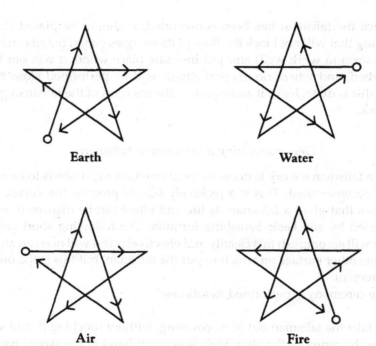

Diagram 8-19. Banishing pentagrams.

A medieval handbook of geomancy

T he following text is an English translation of *Modo judicandi questiones secundum Petrum de Abano Patavinum* ("The method of judging questions according to Pietro d'Abano of Padua"), a Latin textbook of geomancy that appears in a great many manuscripts from the fourteenth, fifteenth, and sixteenth centuries. Unlike most other handbooks of geomancy—medieval as well as modern— it deals entirely with the interpretation of the geomantic chart, and it uses a wide and flexible array of interpretive tools to make sense of the figures and their relationships; many of the methods of interpretation discussed in chapter 4 can be found here, along with some specialized approaches not covered there. More important, though, is the chance to see geomancy at work as it was practiced in its heyday.

Scholarly readers will want to know that the text I have used for this translation is that edited by Therese Charmasson in her important book *Recherces sur une Technique Divinatoire: La Geomancie dans l'Occident Medieval*, based on the copy in Munich, ms. lat. 489, fol. 222–233. Words in square brackets have been added for the sake of clarity.

The method of judging questions according to Pietro d'Abano of Padua

Desiring to give true and certain judgement, according to the glorious and venerable science of geomancy, one first ought to invoke, supplicate and entreat the clemency of omnipotent God, so that one may be able to extract the true significance of the figures, and open up by a true path the occult property of the twelve houses, and the Judge together with the Witnesses. In this judgement, nine things are to be considered:

In the first place, the good or evil character of the figures.

In the second place, to know what are the significators of the question.

In the third place, if the first figure, which signifies the querent, occupies the house of the quesited.

In the fourth place, if the first significator seeks conjunction with the other significator or on the contrary, if the significator of the quesited seeks conjunction with that of the querent.

In the fifth place, to see whether a mutation is made in the question, that is, if either significator shifts out of its proper place, making a conjunction between itself and the other significator.

In the sixth place, to see if there may be any translation between significators.

In the seventh place, the good or evil character of the witnesses and judge must be considered.

In the eighth place, the nature and significance of the sixteenth figure.

In the ninth place, whether a thing lost will arrive quickly or whether hope will be cut off.

Of the good and evil character of the figures. The good or evil character of the figures is considered in this way. Now the good or evil of the four cardinal houses [that is, the first, fourth, seventh and tenth houses of the chart] ought to be considered, namely, which figures are benevolent, because if the figure in the first house is benevolent, a good beginning is to be presumed, whether from the goodness of the querent or otherwise; if the figure in the fourth house is good, a good end is to be rejoiced in; if the figures in the seventh and tenth houses are good, a good middle is to be hoped for, and the reverse has the opposite meaning. And if the fifteenth figure [the Judge] agrees with the fourth, the best end of all is not to be doubted, and the reverse has the opposite meaning.

Of the kinds of figures. Then it must be seen whether good figures are in aspect to the ascendant, because if they are in sextile aspect, that is, in the third and eleventh houses, it is good; if in trine aspect, that is in the fifth and ninth houses, it signifies better than all, and the reverse, when the ascendant is weakened [by unfavorable figures square or opposite the ascendant].

Of the exaltations of the figures. Next the exaltations of the figures must be considered. Now the figures of Mercury, Albus and Conjunctio, are exalted in the ascendant [the first house]; the figures of Luna, Populus and Via, in the third [house]; the figures of Venus, Amissio and Puer, in the fifth; the figures of Mars, Rubeus and Puella, in the sixth; the figures of the Sun, Fortuna Major and Fortuna Minor, in the ninth; the figures of Jupiter, Acquisitio and Laetitia, in the eleventh; the figures of Saturn, Carcer and Tristitia, in the twelfth; and when a good figure is in its exaltation, its good significance is doubled; if it is evil, its evil is doubled.

Of the association of figures. Likewise it must be seen whether a figure benefits from its companions, and from the figures from which it arises. Now if a good figure is in good company [that is, if the figure in the house paired with it is favorable], its good significance is completed and increased, and the reverse has the opposite effect, if it has an evil companion; if on the other hand a good figure is created from good parents, this signifies complete good, while if it is created from one good and another evil figure, it remains in its own proper significance. And if it arises from two evil figures, it is tainted by them and is left mixed in character. If it is evil, all is reversed.

Of the changing of a figure and its significance. It must be known also why a figure is said to change its fortune; this means that it sometimes happens that fortunate signs exercise their significance against the will of the querent, and signify that the thing desired will not arrive. For example: if someone asks whether rains will come, and Laetitia is formed in the tenth house, which is the house of rains or drought, this Laetitia here signifies fair weather and lack of rain; Laetitia therefore changes its fortune, for although it is good, it becomes of evil significance—fair weather—when this is against the desire and will of the querent. For indeed any figure which has a significance against the will of the querent, whatever it may be, in that question is judged evil, and the reverse in the opposite case.

Of knowing how to discover the Significator. Now judgement in geomancy can in no way be given, if the practitioner himself does not know the places of the question, that is, the significators, which are known to signify the success or failure of the subject of the question. For indeed the significators are those figures which signify the querent and the quesited.

First house. Now the place of the querent's significator is the first house, since in the first house the querent is always considered, and note that if someone asks in the place of another, the one for whom the question is asked is said to be the querent, whether he be present or not. For example: if I ask [a question] for N., not I but he is called the querent. The other significator, which signifies the quesited matter, is considered now in one house, now in another.

Second house. If, for example, someone asks if he will profit, or if he will receive money from a debtor, or if something lost is in the house, or if his money will remain untouched, or if he will be enriched, all these are considered in the second house.

Third house. If on the other hand he should ask whether he is loved by a brother or sister, or whether he will die before a brother of his or a sister or a close relative, or of what sort his companions may be in lodgings or on a journey, or if a journey will be short, or if it will be safe, or if his messenger whom he wishes to send will do what he is supposed to do, all of this is considered in the third house; it is the other significator.

Fourth house. And if someone should ask whether he is loved by his father, or by his uncle, or by his father-in-law, or by any older member of his family, or if an inheritance will be increased or recovered, or if it be good to build a castle or a house, or if any work which has been started will come to an end, or if a thing has been lost in the place enquired about, or in what part of a house or ship or land or field a thing has been lost, or if a thing that has been lost will be found in a particular place, or if some building will fall down, or if a plantation of trees will come to bear fruit, or if a field will abound with produce, or if the price of seed will rise or fall in a particular month or year, or if a particular tract of land is fertile, or if any matter will come to a good end; in all these questions, the fourth house is the significator.

Fifth house. And if someone asks whether he will have children, or similarly the querent asks whether she will conceive or give birth, or die during childbirth, or have complications, or what food will be served at a banquet, and of what quality, and if the food will be poisoned, or if the returns from the querent's property will be increased, or if he will live happily, or if a lawsuit or dispute which is carried on against him will be settled peaceably; the fifth house signifies all these things.

Sixth house. In the sixth house, these things are considered, namely whether the querent will be sick, or if an absent person is sick, and what caused him to fall sick; if he will be cured by the medicine which has been selected; if small animals are fruitful or sterile or if they will be lost; if it is good to keep or hire a servant, or if he will run away or serve well, or if he will stay a long time with the querent, or what color the urine will be [this is a sign used in medical diagnosis].

Seventh house. In the seventh house, these things are considered: if the querent will take a wife; if a marriage will take place; if a marriage will be fortunate; if the querent will marry a particular woman; if he will regain a wife or a sweetheart or a lover; if he will be defeated by someone with whom he fights; if a woman be a virgin or if she has given birth; if a wife or sweetheart be faithful; if the querent will separate from his wife; if a particular horse will win a race; if the querent will be defeated in war or in a law-suit; if his adversary will make peace or an alliance with him; if a business partner is honest; if a debtor intends to pay his debt; if an exile will return to his homeland; if the exile will be well in the land to which he goes; of what quality is the land to which he goes; and the quality of all opposites is declared by the seventh house.

Eighth house. In the eighth house, these things are considered: whether someone will die at a predestined point; if the querent will get possession of the remains of the dead; if in the land to which he goes, an exile will become rich; if his adversary has much money; if something reached the person to whom it was sent; if he will die as a result of a particular illness; whether something he fears has truly come upon him.

Ninth house. In the ninth house, these things are asked: if a particular person is Catholic, or if he has faith or if he is religious; if a wise man has skill [or a particular skill or knowledge]; if a long journey will be safe; if a church will be built; if the querent will receive church preferment [appointment to an ecclesiastical office]; if a church which has been begun will be completed; if a church will fall down; if the querent will not receive preferment; if he will be deposed from his position in the church; if a religious official will govern his subordinates well; if the church will receive goods; if the querent will receive favor in the church; if the treasury of the church will be increased; if the church will be honored with riches.

Tenth house. In the tenth house, these things are considered: if the querent will be king or a powerful man or an elected official; if he will be bailiff to a king or official, that is, will have land or people placed under him by the king; if the king will be honored in his kingdom or despised or if he will be deposed; if having been deposed he will regain the throne; if he will govern the kingdom well; if the kingdom will be at peace; if the kingdom will expand; if the querent has hope of gaining honors; if the querent will be honored; if he will be fortunate in his relations with the king or a prince or his particular lord; if the querent's teacher be faithful in all things; if the querent is loved by the king or prince or his lord; if his teacher knows the branch of knowledge which he has promised to teach; if the querent is loved by his mother; how his widowed mother will fare; if he will profit by a manual art; if the manual art about which he asks will be useful and lucrative to him; if on an appointed day it will rain, or what kind of wind will blow, or what kind of weather there will be.

Eleventh house. In the eleventh house, these things are considered: if the querent will be fortunate; if he will have friends; if a friend is useful; if the querent will be helped by a friend; if the friendship of a friend will endure; if a king or prince will have treasure, or if his treasury will increase; if the king's tribute [or taxes] will remain the same; if he will conquer land; from whom he will have tribute; if the querent will be a bailiff or a servant or a minister at the court of a king or prince; if a king or prince will forgive the querent and restore his [position, property, etc.]; if the querent will lose his position as bailiff or servant to a king or prince; if a thing hoped for will come to pass or if the querent will attain a thing hoped for; if by his service he will benefit his elders; if a thing which has been entrusted to someone will be safe, or if a thing which has been deposited will be reclaimed.

Twelfth house. In the twelfth house, these things are considered: whether the querent will have hidden enemies, or if the hidden enemies will be dangerous, or if hidden enemies will defeat the querent; or how hidden enemies seek to harm the querent; and if a large animal which he wants to buy be good or vicious, or if he should sell it, if he will in truth profit from it, or if it is old or young; and if the querent will be captured or imprisoned, or if in that prison he will die, or if he will go into or out of debt or prison or slavery, and if he will be honorably buried, or what kind of sepulcher he will have, and if after his death he will have a good reputation or a bad one.

Of the occupation of figures. Occupation is when the sign of the querent occupies the house of the quesited. For example: someone asked whether he would be able to recover his house, which he had lost, and Albus was in the first house and shifted itself [i.e., also appeared] in the fourth, occupying the place of the quesited. And note that there is no kind of answer in this science better than this one, if the first sign be fortunate, seeing that the thing in question must be acquired, without doubt, if God wills.

Of the conjunction of figures. Conjunction is when one significator shifts itself into conjunction with the other significator [i.e., also appears in a house next to that of the other significator]. For example: someone asked whether his servant who ran away could be recovered, and Acquisitio was in the first house, and shifted itself into the fifth house, that is, in conjunction with the sixth house, which is the significator of the servant; from which one supposes that the servant will be recovered, because of the significance of this conjunction. And note that when the first significator shifts itself into conjunction with the other significator, this always means that the querent, through his own diligence and effort, will acquire the thing inquired about; and when the figure of the quesited goes to a conjunction with the significator of the querent, then this will mean that the querent, without diligence or effort on his own part, will have the thing inquired about.

Of the mutation of significators. Mutation is when both significators shift out of their own places, making a conjunction between themselves. For example: someone asked whether he would be able to make love with the woman he loved, and Carcer was in the first house and Puer in the seventh, signifying the woman; now there is a shifting of Carcer to the fourth house and Puer to the third house. This conjunction of significators outside of their own places means, therefore, that the querent will make love with the woman in question, but not in the proper place, that is, not in the house of the querent, nor in the house of the quesited; but because the conjunction is said to be made from the place of the querent, it denotes that the querent will make love with the woman somewhere near his own home.

Of the translation of figures. Translation is when one figure carries the disposition [of the matter] from one significator to the other. For example: someone asked whether he would be able to get married, and this is how the divination came out: Acquisitio was in the house of the querent and Laetitia was in conjunction with it, making a good translation to the seventh, since it was conjoined to it in the eighth [i.e., Laetitia also appeared in the eighth house and was thus in conjunction with the seventh house, the house of marriage], thus having disposition of the marriage, and because the [sign in the] ascendant was acquisitive and fortunate, and because the figure Conjunctio was formed by [the combination of the figures in] the first and seventh houses, and because a trine aspect from the fifth house strengthened the ascendant, and even more because of the combination of all these, the marriage was brought about with ease (see Diagram A-1).

Of the good or evil character of the Judge and Witnesses. The good or evil character of the Judge and Witnesses is considered thus, as experience shows: since the fifteenth figure [the Judge] is closer to the diviner than the others, it is therefore attributed to the Moon among the planets, since the Moon is closer to the Earth than the other planets. And just as the Moon in one lunation [lunar month], by reason of the very swift speed of its course, passes through every sign and visits all of the planets, moving away from one and approaching another; in the same way, the fifteenth figure comes into being out of the procreation and generation of all the figures above it. But since among these we first have the thirteenth and fourteenth figures [the Witnesses], the thirteenth figure [the Right Witness] is attributed to the planet from which the Moon is moving away, and the fourteenth [the Left Witness] to the one it is approaching; therefore if the thirteenth is good and fourteenth evil, this signifies that the matter about which the question is asked tends to the worse, and if the thirteenth is evil and the fourteenth good, the matter tends to the better, if the fifteenth supports their testimony. The good or evil character of the Judge does not differ from that of the fourth house, because both of them signify the end of the matter in question; from which, if both of them be good, there can be no doubt of the best conclusion of the quesited matter, if God wills, and the reverse in the opposite case; and if one is good and the other evil, you may judge that the quesited matter will have a medium end.

Of the sixteenth figure. The sixteenth figure [i.e., the Reconciler], the good or evil character of which must be considered, is created from the first and fifteenth figures. If it is good, and appears in another part of the chart, it signifies that, after the quesited thing is obtained in whatever position in the chart pertains to it, there will also be that good thing which arises out of the nature of the house in which the sixteenth figure is found. But if it be evil, all is the reverse.

Of the swift or slow conclusion of the question. Whether the success or failure of the thing desired will take place sooner or later is considered thus: count the points of all sixteen figures [in the divination, that is, all the figures including the Reconciler] of which I speak. Then if the number of points be 96, because all the figures of geomancy are formed out of a total of 96 points, it is plain that the arrival of the conclusion will be swift, and neither slow nor doubtful; if it be more than 96, it will be slow, and by as much as it is more than 96, it will be that much slower; and if the tale of the points be less than 96, the quesited matter seeks its end that much more quickly; and by as much as it is less than 96, so much more quickly will the end arrive.

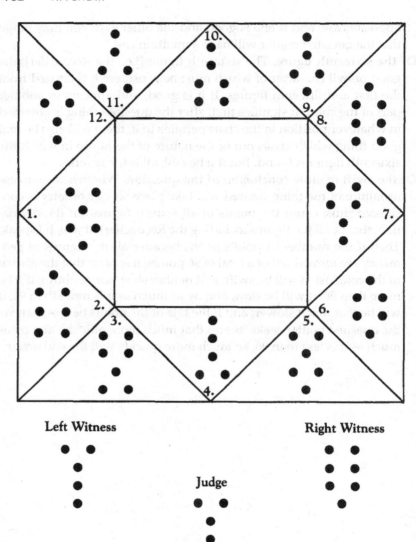

Diagram A–1. A reconstruction of the geomantic chart discussed in *A Medieval Handbook of Geomancy.*

Translator's note. As a help to interpreting the translation above, I have reconstructed the geomantic chart discussed in the text under *Of the translation of figures*. There are several other possible charts that could correspond to the description given, but this one is the closest fit in terms of the interpretation.

Note, first of all, Laetitia in the second and eighth houses making the translation between the querent in the first and the quesited in the seventh. Both the significators are highly favorable figures, and when added together in the usual way they form the figure Conjunctio—the best possible omen for a question involving marriage. Conjunctio is also the Judge, formed out of Tristitia as Right Witness and Caput Draconis as Left Witness; this suggests that the marriage will help the querent move out of a time of unhappiness and into one of new beginnings. Acquisitio, the querent's significator, also passes to the fifth house, trining itself and entering into a sextile aspect with the significator of the quesited.

In case there is any remaining doubt about the positive nature of the chart, the Reconciler can be used to settle it. Acquisitio in the first house, added to the Judge Conjunctio, makes Fortuna Major—not only the most positive figure of the sixteen, but also the significator of the woman the querent hopes to marry. It's no wonder that the marriage was brought about with ease!

BIBLIOGRAPHY

Agrippa, Henry Cornelius, *Three Books of Occult Philosophy*, trans. James Freake, ed. Donald Tyson (St. Paul: Llewellyn, 1993).

Agrippa, Henry Cornelius (pseud.), *Fourth Book of Occult Philosophy* (repr. Kila, Mont.: Kessinger, 1992). Contains Agrippa's On *Geomancy* and Gerard of Cremona's On *Astrological Geomancy*.

Alighieri, Dante, *The Divine Comedy*, trans. H. F. Cary (New York: Collier, 1909).

Anonymous (ed.), *Fasciculus Geomanticus* (Verona: n.p., 1704). Contains Robert Fludd's *De animae intellectualis scientiae, seu Geomantia, Tractatus de Geomantia in Quatuor Libros Divisus* and *De Geomantia Morborum*, with other geomantic texts.

Bascom, William, *Ifa Divination: Communication Between Gods and Men in West Africa* (Bloomington: Indiana UP, 1969).

Charmasson, Therese, *Recherces sur une Technique Divinatoire: La Geomancie dans l'Occident Medieval* (Geneva: Librairie Droz, 1980). Contains the text of *Modo Judicandi Questiones Secundum Petrum de Abano Patavinum.*

Heninger, S. K. Jr., *Touches of Sweet Harmony: Pythagorean Cosmology and Renaissance Poetics* (San Marino, Calif.: Huntington Library, 1974).

Heydon, John, *Theomagia, or the Temple of Wisdome* (London: for Henry Brome at the Gun in Ivie-Lane, and for Thomas Rooks at the Lambe at the east end of St. Pauls, 1664).

185

Hulse, David Allen, *The Key Of It All, Book Two: The Western Mysteries* (St. Paul: Llewellyn, 1994).

The I Ching or Book of Changes, trans. Richard Wilhelm and Cary F. Baynes (Princeton: Princeton University Press, 1967).

Jaulin, Robert, *La Geomancie: Analyse Formelle* (Paris: Mouton, 1966).

Josten, C. H., "Robert Fludd's Theory of Geomancy and his Experiences at Avignon in the Winter of 1601 to 1602," *Journal of the Warburg and Courtauld Institutes 27* (1964), pp. 327–335.

Lessa, William, A., "Divining Knots in the Carolines," *Journal of the Polynesian Society 68* (1959), pp. 188–204.

Pennick, Nigel, *Games of the Gods* (York Beach, Maine: Weiser, 1989).

Regardie, Israel, A *Practical Guide to Geomantic Divination* (New York: Samuel Weiser, 1972).

_____, *The Complete Golden Dawn System of Magic* (Phoenix: Falcon, 1984).

_____, *The Golden Dawn* (St. Paul: Llewellyn, 1971).

Schwei, Priscilla, and Ralph Pestka, *The Complete Book of Astrological Geomancy* (St. Paul: Llewellyn, 1990).

Skinner, Stephen, *The Oracle of Geomancy* (Bridport, Dorset: Prism, 1986).

_____, *Terrestrial Astrology* (London: Routledge & Kegan Paul, 1980).

INDEX

Abano, Pietro d', 9, 173, 174
Acquisitio, 7, 42–43, 64, 71–2, 73, 74, 76,
    90, 108, 156
Africa, 10, 11
agbigba divination, 11
Agiel, 117
Agrippa, Henry Cornelius, 5, 9, 25
Albus, 6, 31–32, 70, 77, 84–85, 106, 107,
    108, 143, 155
Amissio, 6, 29–30, 64, 73, 77, 86, 88, 99,
    108, 143, 155
amulet(s), 164
anima mundi, 15, 58
astrology, 5, 17

Bartzabel, 117
binary numbers, 9–10
buried treasure, 110–112

Cabalistic Cross, 120, 121–122, 125, 131
Caput Draconis, 7, 49, 77, 84, 88, 90, 92,
    112, 158, 183

Carcer, 7, 44, 64, 70, 73, 74, 84, 99, 106,
    108, 157, 179
Cauda Draconis, 7, 48, 69, 74, 80, 86,
    90–92, 98, 157
Charmasson, Therese, 173
Chashmodai, 118
China, 10
color(s), 25–26
company of houses, 93–95
competitions, 106–109
Conjunctio, 6, 37–38, 64, 69, 71, 73, 77,
    90, 92, 102, 106, 108, 156, 183
conjunction, 81–83, 174, 179
consecration, ritual of, 133–136,
    167–171
corpus mundi, 16
correspondences, 20

Dante, 13
dates and times, discovering, 101
Daughters, Four, 60–61, 64, 73, 74–75,
    79, 95

187

deconsecration, ceremony of, 172–173
dreams, 105

element(s), 20–21, 24–25

feng shui, 3
Fludd, Robert, 5, 13
fluid condenser, 159–160
Fortuna Major, 6, 35–36, 64, 71–2, 73,
        84, 92, 108, 112, 155, 183
Fortuna Minor, 8, 50–51, 64, 73, 77,
        83–84, 88, 107, 108, 112, 158
fourfold breath, 141–142

Gerard of Cremona, 9
Golden Dawn, Hermetic Order of the,
        8, 22, 26, 120, 130, 151
Graphiel, 117

Hagiel, 118
hakata divination, 11
Hermes Trismegistus, 13
Heydon, John, 5, 8, 9, 22
Hismael, 117
Holy Grail, 28
houses, twelve, 77–79, 176–179
Hugh of Santalla, 9

I Ching, 10, 11
Ifa oracle, 11, 19
'ilm al-raml, 12

Judge, 63, 64, 68–69, 72, 74, 77, 95, 180
Jung, Carl, 14

karma, 153
Kedemel, 118
khat al-raml, 12

Laetitia, 7, 47, 69, 76, 77, 81, 90–92, 107,
        108, 157, 183
Leibniz, G. W., 10
Lesser Banishing Ritual of the
        Pentagram, 120, 122–123, 125,
        131, 137
ley lines, 3

locating persons, 96–7
lost objects, 99

magic, 17, 20, 59, 116–125, 127–128,
        151–172
Malkah be-Tarshishim ve-ad Ruachoth
        Shechalim, 118
meditation, 139–144, 146–148
mutation, 83–84, 174, 179–180
Mothers, Four, 60, 64, 73, 74–75, 79, 95

Nakhiel, 117
natural magic, 127
news and rumors, checking, 105
Nieces, Four, 61–63, 73, 74–75, 79, 95

occultism, 4, 20, 115
occupation, 80–81, 174, 179

Patrizzi, Francisco, 13
planet(s), 23
Planetary Spirit(s), 117–119, 120, 123,
        124
Populus, 6, 33–34, 64, 73, 85, 90, 92, 105,
        106, 108, 112, 155
projection of points, 92–93
Puella, 6, 39–40, 70, 74, 77, 82, 98, 99,
        108, 156
Puer, 6, 27–28, 74, 76, 77, 106, 108, 143,
        154, 179

querent, 80, 174, 176
quesited, 80, 174
question(s) for divination, 55–56

randomness, 14
reconciler, 90–92, 181
ritual magic, 128
Rubeus, 7, 41, 74, 80, 86, 96, 106,
        108, 156

scrying in the spirit vision, 144–150
Shad Barshemoth ha-Shartathan, 118
sigil ritual of air, 162
sigil ritual of earth, 163–4
sigil ritual of fire, 161

sigil ritual of water, 162–163
sigils, geomantic, 154–158
significator(s), 80, 174, 179
sikidy oracle, 12
Sorath, 117
spiritus mundi, 16
synchronicity, 14

talisman(s), 12, 164–167
Taphthartharath, 118
Thorndyke, Lynn, 12
Tiriel, 118
translation, 84–85, 174, 180
traveling, 106
triplicities, four, 74–77
Tristitia, 7, 45–46, 77, 90, 106, 108, 109,
    157, 183

unknown person(s), 96

Via, 8, 52–53, 64, 73, 82–83, 86, 88, 99,
    105, 108, 112, 158
vibration, 120, 130

Way of the Points, 72–74, 77
weather, 109–110
Witnesses, 63, 68–69, 73, 74, 95, 180
working tool(s), 164

Yophiel, 117

Zazel, 117
zodiac, 24

The shield chart.

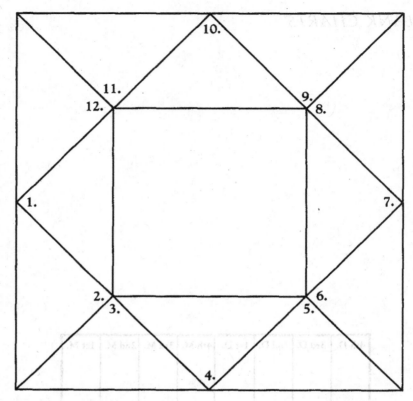

The geomantic house chart.